TIMED READINGS PLUS

25 Two-Part Lessons
with Questions for
Building Reading Speed and Comprehension

BOOK ONE

Edward Spargo

JAMESTOWN  PUBLISHERS

a division of NTC/CONTEMPORARY PUBLISHING GROUP
Lincolnwood, Illinois USA

Timed Readings Plus, Book One, Level D
Selection text adapted from Compton's Encyclopedia.
Used with permission of Compton's Learning Company.

ISBN: 0-89061-903-4

Published by Jamestown Publishers,
a division of NTC/Contemporary Publishing Group, Inc.,
4255 West Touhy Avenue,
Lincolnwood, Illinois, 60646 U.S.A.
©1998 by NTC/Contemporary Publishing Group, Inc.
90 ML 09876543

CONTENTS

To the Instructor

Overview

Timed Readings Plus is designed to develop both reading speed and comprehension. A timed selection in each lesson focuses on improving reading rate. A nontimed selection—the "plus" selection—follows the timed selection. The nontimed selection concentrates on building mastery in critical areas of comprehension.

The 10 books in the series span reading levels 4–13, with one book at each level. Readability of the selections was assessed by using the Fry Readability Scale. Each book contains 25 lessons; each lesson is divided into Parts A and B.

Part A includes the timed selection followed by 10 multiple-choice questions: 5 fact questions and 5 thought questions. The timed selection is 400 words long and contains subject matter that is factual, nonfiction, and textbook-like. Because everyone—regardless of level—reads a 400-word passage, the steps for the timed selection can be concurrent for everyone.

Part B includes the nontimed selection, which is more narrative than the timed selection. The length of the selection varies depending on the subject matter, which relates to the content of the timed selection. The nontimed selection is followed by five comprehension questions that address the following major comprehension skills: recognizing words in context, distinguishing fact from opinion, keeping events in order, making correct inferences, and understanding main ideas.

Getting Started

Begin by assigning students to a level. A student should start with a book that is one level below his or her current reading level. If a student's reading level is not known, a suitable starting point would be one or two levels below the student's present grade in school.

Teaching a Lesson: Part A

Work in each lesson begins with the timed selection in Part A. If you wish to have all the students in the class read a selection at the same time, you can coordinate the timing using the following method. Give students the signal to preview. Allow 15 seconds for this. Have students begin reading the selection at the same time. After one minute has passed, write on the chalkboard the time that has elapsed. Update the time at 10-second intervals (1:00, 1:10, 1:20, etc.). Tell students to copy down the last time shown on the chalkboard when they finish reading. They should then record this reading time in the space designated after the selection.

If students keep track of their own reading times, have them write the times at which they start and finish reading on a separate piece of paper and then figure and record their reading time as above.

Students should now answer the ten questions that follow the Part A selection. Responses are recorded by putting an X in the box next to the student's choice of answer. Correct responses to eight or more questions indicates satisfactory comprehension and recall.

Teaching a Lesson: Part B

When students have finished Part A, they can move on to read the Part B selection. Although brief, these selections deliver all the content needed to attack the range of comprehension questions that follow.

Students next answer the comprehension questions that follow the Part B selection. Directions for answering the questions are provided with each question. Correct responses require deliberation and discrimination.

Correcting and Scoring Answers

Using the Answer Key at the back of the book, students self-score their responses to the questions in Parts A and B. Incorrect answers should be circled and the correct answers should be marked. The number of correct answers for Part A and for Part B and the total correct answers should be tallied on the final page of the lesson.

Using the Graphs

Reading times are plotted on the Reading Rate graph at the back of the book. The legend on the graph automatically converts reading times to words-per-minute rates. Comprehension totals are plotted on the Comprehension Scores graph. Plotting automatically converts the raw scores to a comprehension percentage based on four points per correct answer.

Diagnosis and Evaluation

The Comprehension Skills Profile graph at the back of the book tracks student responses to the Part B comprehension questions. For each incorrect response, students should mark an X in the corresponding box on the graph. A column of Xs rising above other columns indicates a specific comprehension weakness. Using the profile, you can assess trends in student performance and suggest remedial work if necessary.

A student who has reached a peak in reading speed (with satisfactory comprehension) is ready to advance to the next book in the series. Before moving on to the next book, students should be encouraged to maintain their speed and comprehension on a number of lessons in order to consolidate their achievement.

HOW TO USE THIS BOOK

Getting Started

Study Part A: Reading Faster and Better. Read and learn the steps to follow and the techniques to use to help you read more quickly and more efficiently.

Study Part B: Mastering Reading Comprehension. Learn what the five categories of comprehension are all about. Knowing what kind of comprehension response is expected from you and how to achieve that response will help you better comprehend all you read.

Working a Lesson

Find the Starting Lesson. Locate the timed selection in Part A of the lesson that you are going to read. Wait for your instructor's signal to preview the selection. Your instructor will allow you 15 seconds for previewing.

Read the Part A Selection. When your instructor gives you the signal, begin reading. Read at a faster-than-normal speed. Read carefully so that you will be able to answer questions about what you have read.

Record Your Reading Time. When you finish reading, look at the blackboard and note your reading time. Write this time at the bottom of the page on the line labeled Reading Time.

Answer the Part A Questions. Answer the 10 questions that follow the selection. There are 5 fact questions and 5 thought questions. Choose the best answer to each question and put an X in that box.

Read the Part B Selection. This passage is less textbook-like and more story-like than the timed selection. Read well enough so that you can answer the questions that follow.

Answer the Part B Questions. These questions are different from traditional multiple-choice questions. In answering these questions, you must make three choices for each question. Instructions for answering each category of question are given. There are 15 responses for you to record.

Correct Your Answers. Use the Answer Key at the back of the book. For the Part A questions, circle any wrong answer and put an X in the box you should have marked. For the Part B questions, circle any wrong answer and write the correct letter or number next to it.

Scoring Your Work

Total Your Correct Answers. Count your correct answers for Part A and for Part B. Record those numbers on the appropriate lines at the end of the lesson. Then add the two scores to determine your total correct answers. Record that number on the appropriate line.

Plotting Your Progress

Plot Your Reading Time. Refer to the Reading Rate graph on page 116. On the vertical line that represents your lesson, put an X at the point where it intersects your reading time, shown along the left-hand side. The right-hand side of the graph will reveal your words-per-minute reading speed. Your instructor will review this graph from time to time to evaluate your progress.

Plot Your Comprehension Scores. Record your comprehension scores on the graph on page 117. On the vertical line that represents your lesson, put an X at the point where it intersects your total correct answers, shown along the left-hand side. The right-hand side of the graph will reveal your comprehension percentage. Your instructor will want to review this graph, too. Your achievement, as shown on both graphs, will determine your readiness to move on to higher and more challenging levels.

Plot Your Comprehension Skills. You will find the Comprehension Skills Profile on page 118. It is used to record your wrong answers only for the Part B questions. The five categories of questions are listed along the bottom. There are five columns of boxes, one column for each question. For every wrong answer, put an X in a box for that question. Your instructor will use this graph to detect any comprehension problems you may be experiencing.

PART A: READING FASTER AND BETTER

Step 1: Preview

When you read, do you start in with the first word, or do you look over the whole selection for a moment? Good readers preview the selection first. This helps make them good—and fast—readers. Here are the steps to follow when previewing the timed selection in Part A of each unit.

1. Read the Title. Titles are designed not only to announce the subject, but also to make the reader think. What can you learn from the title? What thoughts does it bring to mind? What do you already know about this subject?

2. Read the First Sentence. Read the first two sentences if they are short. The opening sentence is the writer's opportunity to greet the reader. Some writers announce what they hope to tell you in the selection. Some writers tell you why they are writing. Other writers just try to get your attention.

3. Read the Last Sentence. Read the final two sentences if they are short. The closing sentence is the writer's last chance to talk to you. Some writers repeat the main idea once more. Some writers draw a conclusion—this is what they have been leading up to. Other writers summarize their thoughts; they tie all the facts together.

4. Scan the Selection. Glance through the selection quickly to see what else you can pick up. Look for anything that can help you read the selection. Are there names, dates, or numbers? If so, you may have to read more slowly. Is the selection informative—containing a lot of facts, or is it conversational—an informal discussion with the reader?

Step 2: Read for Meaning

When you read, do you just see words? Are you so occupied reading words that you sometimes fail to get the meaning? Good readers see beyond the words—they seek the meaning. This makes them faster readers.

1. Build Concentration. You cannot read with understanding if you are not concentrating. When you discover that your thoughts are straying, correct the situation right away. Avoid distractions and distracting situations. Keep the preview information in mind. This will help focus your attention on the selection.

2. Read in Thought Groups. A reader should strive to see words in meaningful combinations. If you see only a word at a time (called word-by-word reading), your comprehension suffers along with your speed.

3. Question the Writer. To sustain the pace you have set for yourself, and to maintain a high level of concentration and comprehension, question the writer as you read. Ask yourself such questions as, "What does this mean? How can I use this information?"

Step 3: Grasp Paragraph Sense

The paragraph is the basic unit of meaning. If you can discover quickly and understand the main point of each paragraph, you can comprehend the writer's message. Good readers know how to find the main ideas quickly. This helps make them faster readers.

1. Find the Topic Sentence. The topic sentence, which contains the main idea, is often the first sentence of a paragraph. It is followed by sentences that support, develop, or explain the main idea. Sometimes a topic sentence comes at the end of a paragraph. When it does, the supporting details come first, building the base for the topic sentence. Some paragraphs do not have a topic sentence; all of the sentences combine to create a meaningful idea.

2. Understand Paragraph Structure. Every well-written paragraph has a purpose. The purpose may be to inform, define, explain, illustrate, and so on. The purpose should always relate to the main idea and expand on it. As you read each paragraph, see how the body of the paragraph is used to tell you more about the main idea.

Step 4: Organize Facts

When you read, do you tend to see a lot of facts without any apparent connection or relationship? Understanding how the facts all fit together to deliver the writer's message is, after all, the reason for reading. Good readers organize facts as they read. This helps them read rapidly and well.

1. Discover the Writer's Plan. Every writer has a plan or outline to follow. If you can discover the writer's method of organization, you have a key to understanding the message. Sometimes the writer gives you obvious signals. The statement, "There are three reasons . . .," should prompt you to look for a listing of the three items. Other less obvious signal words such as *moreover, otherwise,* and *consequently* tell you the direction the writer is taking in delivering a message.

2. Relate as You Read. As you read the selection, keep the information learned during the preview in mind. See how the writer is attempting to piece together a meaningful message. As you discover the relationship among the ideas, the message comes through quickly and clearly.

Part B: Mastering Reading Comprehension

Recognizing Words in Context

Always check to see if the words around a new word—its context—can give you some clue to its meaning. A word generally appears in a context related to its meaning. If the words *soil* and *seeds* appear in an article about gardens, for example, you can assume they are related to the topic of gardens.

Suppose you are unsure of the meaning of the word *expired* in the following paragraph:

> Vera wanted to take a book out, but her library card had expired.
> She had to borrow mine because she didn't have time to renew hers.

You could begin to figure out the meaning of *expired* by asking yourself, "What could have happened to Vera's library card that would make her have to borrow someone else's card?" You might realize that if she had to renew her card, it must have come to an end or run out. This would lead you to conclude that the word *expired* must mean to come to an end or run out. You would be right. The context suggested the meaning to you.

Context can also affect the meaning of a word you know. The word *key*, for instance, has many meanings. There are musical keys, door keys, and keys to solving a mystery. The context in which *key* occurs will tell you which meaning is right.

Sometimes a hard word will be explained by the words that immediately follow it. The word *grave* in the following sentence might give you trouble:

> He looked grave; there wasn't a trace of a smile on his lips.

You can figure out that the second part of the sentence explains the word *grave:* "wasn't a trace of a smile" indicates a serious look, so *grave* must mean serious.

The subject of a sentence and your knowledge about that subject might also help you determine the meaning of an unknown word. Try to decide the meaning of the word *revive* in the following sentence:

> Sunshine and water will revive those drooping plants.

The sentence is about giving plants light and water. You may know that plants need light and water to be healthy. If you know that drooping plants are not healthy, you can figure out that *revive* means to bring back to health.

Distinguishing Fact from Opinion

Every day you are called upon to sort out fact and opinion. When a friend says she saw Mel Gibson's greatest movie last night, she is giving you her opinion. When she says she saw Mel Gibson's latest movie, she may be stating a fact. The fact can be proved—you can check to confirm or verify that the movie is indeed Mel Gibson's most recent film. The opinion can be disputed—ask around and others may not agree about the film's unqualified greatness. Because much of what you read and hear contains both facts and opinions, you need to be able to tell them apart. You need the skill of distinguishing fact from opinion.

Facts are statements that can be proved true. The proof must be objective and verifiable. You must be able to check for yourself to confirm a fact.

Look at the following facts. Notice that they can be checked for accuracy and confirmed. Suggested sources for verification appear in parentheses.

- In 1998 Bill Clinton was president of the United States. (Consult newspapers, news broadcasts, election results, etc.)

- Earth revolves around the sun. (Look it up in encyclopedias or astrological journals; ask knowledgeable people.)

- Dogs walk on four legs. (See for yourself.)

Opinions are statements that cannot be proved true. There is no objective evidence you can consult to check the truthfulness of an opinion. Unlike facts, opinions express personal beliefs or judgments. Opinions reveal how someone feels about a subject, not the facts about that subject. You might agree or disagree with someone's opinion, but you cannot prove it right or wrong.

Look at the following opinions. Reasons for classification as opinions appear in parentheses.

- Bill Clinton was born to be a president. (You cannot prove this by referring to birth records. There is no evidence to support this belief.)

- Intelligent life exists on other planets in our solar system. (There is no proof of this. It may be proved true some day, but for now it is just an educated guess—not a fact.)

- Dog is man's best friend. (This is not a fact; your best friend might not be a dog.)

As you read, be aware that facts and opinions are frequently mixed together. The following passage contains both facts and opinions:

> The new 2000 Cruising Yacht offers lots of real-life interior room. It features a luxurious aft cabin, not some dim "cave." The galley

comes equipped with a full-size refrigerator and freezer. And this spacious galley has room to spare. The heads (there are two) have separate showers. The fit and finish are beyond equal and the performance is responsive and outstanding.

Did you detect that the third and fifth sentences state facts and that the rest of the sentences express opinions? Both facts and opinions are useful to you as a reader. But to evaluate what you read and to read intelligently, you need to know the difference between them.

Keeping Events in Order

Writers organize details in a pattern. They present information in a certain order. Recognizing how writers organize—and understanding that organization—can help you improve your comprehension.

When details are arranged in the precise order in which they occurred, a writer is using a chronological (or time) pattern. A writer may, however, change this order. The story may "flash back" to past events that affected the present. The story may "flash forward" to show the results of present events. The writer may move back and forth between past, present, and future to help you see the importance of events.

Making Correct Inferences

Much of what you read suggests more than it says. Writers do not always state outright what they want you to know. Frequently, they omit information that underlies the statements they make. They may assume that you already know it. They may want you to make the effort to figure out the implied information. To get the most out of what you read, you must come to an understanding about unstated information. You can do this through inference. From what is stated, you make inferences about what is not.

You make many inferences every day. Imagine, for example, that you are visiting a friend's house for the first time. You see a bag of dog food. You infer (make an inference) that the family has a dog. On another day you overhear a conversation. You catch the names of two actors and the words *scene, dialogue,* and *directing.* You infer that the people are discussing a movie or play.

In these situations and others like them, you infer unstated information from what you observe or read. Readers who cannot make inferences cannot see beyond the obvious. For the careful reader, facts are just the beginning. Facts stimulate your mind to think beyond them—to make an inference about what is meant but not stated.

The following passage is about Charles Dickens. As you read it, see how many inferences you can make.

Charles Dickens visited the United States in 1867. Wherever he went, the reception was the same. The night before, crowds arrived and lined up before the door. By morning the streets were campgrounds, with men, women, and children sitting or sleeping on blankets. Hustlers got ten times the price of a ticket. Once inside, audiences were surprised to hear their favorite Dickens characters speak with an English accent. After 76 readings Dickens boarded a ship for England. When his fellow passengers asked him to read, he said he'd rather be put in irons!

Did you notice that many inferences may be drawn from the passage? Dickens attracted huge crowds. From that fact you can infer that he was popular. His English accent surprised audiences. You can infer that many people didn't know he was English. Hustlers got high prices for tickets. This suggests that "scalping" tickets is not new. Dickens refused to read on the ship. You can infer that he was exhausted and tired of reading aloud to audiences. Those are some obvious inferences that can be made from the passage. More subtle ones can also be made; however, if you see the obvious ones, you understand how inferences are made.

Be careful about the inferences you make. One set of facts may suggest several inferences. Not all of them will be correct; some will be faulty inferences. The correct inference is supported by enough evidence to make it more likely than other inferences.

Understanding Main Ideas

The main idea tells who or what is the subject of the paragraph or passage. The main idea is the most important idea, the idea that provides purpose and direction. The rest of the paragraph or passage explains, develops, or supports the main idea. Without a main idea, there would be only a collection of unconnected thoughts. It would be like a handle and a bowl without the "idea cup," or bread and meat without the "idea sandwich."

In the following passage, the main idea is printed in italics. As you read, observe how the other sentences develop or explain the main idea.

Typhoon Chris hit with full fury today on the central coast of Japan. Heavy rain from the storm flooded the area. High waves carried many homes into the sea. People now fear that the heavy rains will cause mudslides in the central part of the country. The number of people killed by the storm may climb past the 200 mark by Saturday.

In this paragraph, the main idea statement appears first. It is followed by sentences that explain, support, or give details. Sometimes the main idea appears at the end of a paragraph. Writers often construct that type of paragraph when their purpose is to persuade or convince. Readers may be more open to a new idea if the reasons for it are presented first. As you read the following paragraph, think about the overall impact of the supporting ideas. Their purpose is to convince the reader that the main idea in the last sentence should be accepted.

> Last week there was a head-on collision at Huntington and Canton streets. Just a month ago a pedestrian was struck there. Fortunately, she was only slightly injured. In the past year there have been more accidents there than at any other corner in the city. In fact, nearly 10 percent of all city accidents occur there. This intersection is dangerous, and a traffic signal should be installed there before a life is lost.

The details in the paragraph progress from least important to most important. They achieve their full effect in the main idea statement at the end.

In many cases, the main idea is not expressed in a single sentence. The reader is called upon to interpret all of the ideas expressed and decide upon a main idea. Read the following paragraph:

> The American author Jack London was once a pupil at the Cole Grammar School in Oakland, California. Each morning the class sang a song. When the teacher noticed that Jack wouldn't sing, she sent him to the principal. He returned to class with a note. It said that he could be excused from singing if he would write an essay every morning.

In this paragraph, the reader has to interpret the individual ideas and decide on a main idea. This main idea seems reasonable: Jack London's career as a writer began with a "punishment" in grammar school.

Understanding the concept of the main idea and knowing how to find it is important. Transferring that understanding to your reading and study is also important.

Predicting Weather

At one time or another, everyone has stopped to think about the weather. Some days the weather is good. Some days the weather is bad. Still, there are days when the weather seems to change from hour to hour. A day that starts out fine might not keep its promise. Sometimes a day that seems bad turns out better than you thought it would.

There are ways of understanding the weather. One way is to study the clouds. No two clouds are ever alike. But it is still possible to group clouds and to give them names. You can learn to recognize the different kinds of clouds and watch them move across the sky.

As a rule, the higher the clouds, the better the weather, and the lower the clouds, the worse the weather is likely to be. To predict the weather, you should look for three things about clouds: movement, color, and change.

Clouds can tell you if a storm is on the way. For example, cirrus clouds are high, thin, and airy clouds. They can become thick and move lower. This means rain is on the way. Cumulus clouds are puffy clouds that look like balls of cotton. If they get bigger early in the day, then you know it will rain. If there's a sudden, cool breeze and a dark thundercloud appears, then a storm is about to break out.

Clouds are not only signs of storms and rain. They may also be signs of good weather. The cirrus clouds may stay high in the sky and move very slowly. This means fine weather. Fair-weather cumulus clouds are another sign of good weather.

Colors in the sky tell us about the weather, too. A golden ring around the moon tells us that a storm is on the way. A watery, yellow sunset is a sign that rain may be near.

A rainbow has a message, too. The colors of the rainbow come from sun rays shining through falling rain. If you see the sun in the east and a rainbow in the west, the rain may be coming your way. If the sun is in the west and the rainbow is in the east, the rain will be moving away from you.

Clouds are a sign of changing weather. So are the colors in the sky. Knowing a little about them both can help you become weather wise.

Reading Time _1 minute_
_2:24 m._

13

Recalling Facts

1. As a rule, the higher the clouds, the
   - ❏ a. worse the weather.
   - ☑ b. better the weather.
   - ❏ c. colder the weather.

2. Weather can be predicted by observing
   - ❏ a. the colors of a rainbow.
   - ☑ b. cloud movement, color, and change.
   - ❏ c. the height of the sun.

3 Cirrus clouds are
   - ❏ a. puffy white.
   - ☑ b. thin and airy.
   - ❏ c. thunderclouds.

4. High, slow-moving cirrus clouds indicate
   - ❏ a. rain.
   - ❏ b. changing weather.
   - ☑ c. good weather.

5. A storm is on the way if
   - ☑ a. a golden ring is around the moon.
   - ❏ b. a rainbow is in the east and the sun is in the west.
   - ❏ c. a cloud covers the moon.

Understanding Ideas

6. You can conclude from the article that weather prediction
   - ❏ a. is a guessing game.
   - ❏ b. is an exact science.
   - ☑ c. can be based on signs in nature.

7. You can conclude that knowing the weather is
   - ❏ a. of little interest to most people.
   - ☑ b. a concern for many people.
   - ❏ c. a waste of time.

8. You can conclude that cloud names
   - ☑ a. are based on different characteristics.
   - ❏ b. are based on mythical characters.
   - ❏ c. change as the weather changes.

9. It is likely that most severe storms
   - ❏ a. are never predictable.
   - ❏ b. arrive without warning.
   - ☑ c. can be predicted.

10. If cirrus clouds become thick and move lower, you should probably
   - ☑ a. carry an umbrella.
   - ❏ b. expect cool weather.
   - ❏ c. be able to enjoy the outdoors.

"I don't know if we should go camping," Nick said, examining the high, wispy clouds. "Look at that sky."

Jonathan was busy packing their gear into the car. "The radio forecast was for clear weather," he said. "We should go." Nick shrugged and threw his rain gear in the backseat.

By the time they reached the campsite, the thin, wispy clouds had increased and thickened, covering the sky with a blanket of whitish gray. The clouds also looked lower.

"It's going to rain," Nick said. "It's not too late to go back."

"It'll probably be just a shower," Jonathan replied.

"I don't know," Nick responded. "See how dark the sky is getting. Those clouds over there look like sheets of fish scales. My grandfather always said, 'Mares' tails and mackerel scales make lofty ships carry low sails.'"

"Whatever that means," Jonathan replied.

"It means," Nick answered, "that it's going to rain for a long time." As Nick worried, Jonathan began putting up the tent.

By evening it was raining—a slow, steady drizzle. Jonathan and Nick woke up to a heavy rain. The damp, chilled campers hauled their wet tent and soggy sleeping bags home. "Next time," said Jonathan, "I'm going to listen to you instead of the radio."

1. Recognizing Words in Context

Find the word *steady* in the passage. One definition below is a *synonym* for that word; it means the same or almost the same thing. One definition is an *antonym;* it has the opposite or nearly opposite meaning. The other has a completely different meaning. Label the definitions S for *synonym,* A for *antonym,* and D for *different.*

S a. constant

A b. irregular

D c. calm

2. Distinguishing Fact from Opinion

Two of the statements below present *facts*, which can be proved correct. The other statement is an *opinion*, which expresses someone's thoughts or beliefs. Label the statements F for *fact* and O for *opinion.*

F a. There were high, wispy clouds in the sky.

O b. Jonathan should have listened to what Nick said about the clouds.

F c. The radio forecast predicted clear weather.

3. Keeping Events in Order

Two of the statements below describe events that happened at the same time. The other statement describes an event that happened before or after those events. Label them S for *same time,* B for *before,* and A for *after.*

_S_ a. Jonathan and Nick reached the campsite.

_S_ b. The clouds had increased and thickened.

_A_ c. Rain fell in a slow, steady drizzle.

4. Making Correct Inferences

Two of the statements below are correct *inferences,* or reasonable guesses. They are based on information in the passage. The other statement is an incorrect, or faulty, inference. Label the statements C for *correct* inference and F for *faulty* inference.

_C_ a. Studying clouds can give a clue to the weather.

_F_ b. There is no good way to tell whether it will rain or not.

_C_ c. There is some truth to old sayings about weather.

5. Understanding Main Ideas

One of the statements below expresses the main idea of the passage. One statement is too general, or too broad. The other explains only part of the passage; it is too narrow. Label the statements M for *main idea,* B for *too broad,* and N for *too narrow.*

_M_ a. Although Nick thinks it will rain, Jonathan does not listen, and the boys end up camping in the rain.

_B_ b. One way of understanding weather is to study clouds.

_N_ c. The radio forecast was for clear weather, so Jonathan decided to go ahead with the camping trip.

Correct Answers, Part A _____

Correct Answers, Part B _____

Total Correct Answers _____

The Spider

A spider is a small, eight-legged animal. Spiders are best known for the silk they spin. They use their silk to catch large and small insects, their main food.

Many spiders make webs with their threads of silk. They use the webs as traps. If you look closely at a web, you can see the pretty patterns the spider makes. But some spiders do not make webs. One kind of spider jumps onto an insect. Another spider uses its silk like a fishing line. It swings the line until it catches a bug. Then it reels up the line to eat its catch.

Spiders look like many of the insects they eat. But they are not insects. Spiders belong to a group called arachnids. All arachnids have eight legs. None of them have feelers, and none have wings. Mites and ticks belong to this class of animals.

Spiders lay eggs. Some large spiders lay 2,000 eggs at a time. One small spider lays just one egg. Many spiders die after they lay their eggs. The babies must learn to take care of themselves.

A lot of people are afraid of spiders, but only a few spiders can hurt humans. In fact, spiders are very helpful. They get rid of many harmful pests.

A tarantula is a kind of spider. It is large and hairy. Once people thought that a tarantula's bite could give a person a terrible disease. Someone bitten by the tarantula might jump into the air. He or she might make strange noises. But this belief is not true.

You can find tarantulas in many warm climates including the American Southwest. American tarantulas lead fairly quiet lives. These spiders cannot hurt you any more than a bee can.

Some spiders are very dangerous. The black widow is one of these spiders. Its bite is extremely painful. The bite can make you sick for a long time. Only the female black widow can hurt you. She has a shiny black body. It is about the size of a pea. Her long legs are very thin. If you turn her over, you can see a red or yellow mark on her body. But don't try to turn this spider over!

You can find black widows in almost every state. She often makes her webs in dark corners. This spider will not attack you. She will bite only if you bother her.

Reading Time _____

Recalling Facts

1. Spiders are best known for
   - ❏ a. spinning silk.
   - ❏ b. laying eggs.
   - ❏ c. their dangerous bite.

   a

2. Spiders are considered
   - ❏ a. insects.
   - ❏ b. mammals.
   - ❏ c. arachnids.

   c

3. Spiders are helpful because they
   - ❏ a. eat plants.
   - ❏ b. get rid of harmful pests.
   - ❏ c. cure diseases.

   b

4. A very dangerous spider is the
   - ❏ a. tarantula.
   - ❏ b. jumping spider.
   - ❏ c. black widow.

   c

5. Arachnids are animals with
   - ❏ a. four legs.
   - ❏ b. six legs.
   - ❏ c. eight legs.

   c

Understanding Ideas

6. The article suggests that spiders
   - ❏ a. are very dangerous.
   - ❏ b. do not deserve their bad reputation.
   - ❏ c. should not be touched.

   b

7. You can conclude from the article that most spiders get their food by
   - ❏ a. jumping on an insect.
   - ❏ b. biting an insect.
   - ❏ c. trapping them in their silk.

   c

8. You can conclude that spiders differ from insects in part because of their
   - ❏ a. number of legs.
   - ❏ b. egg laying.
   - ❏ c. size.

   a

9. A bite by an American tarantula is likely to
   - ❏ a. be not very harmful.
   - ❏ b. cause death.
   - ❏ c. cause illness.

   a

10. You can conclude that if a spider dies after laying her eggs,
   - ❏ a. the eggs will not hatch.
   - ❏ b. babies that hatch will most likely die.
   - ❏ c. the babies can survive on their own.

   c

A Close Call

The Shepard family had been vacationing in Mexico. Kate and Phil were packing their car for the trip home to Arizona. Suddenly, their young son Mike began crying. He ran to Kate, holding his finger out. "What's wrong, honey?" Kate asked. She looked at his finger. She couldn't see any mark. "I think he's just overtired, Phil," she said to her husband. "Let's get going. I bet he'll sleep all the way home."

Mike didn't sleep, though. Before long, his crying turned to screaming. Then he began throwing up. Now the Shepherds were worried. "We've got to get him to a doctor!" Kate said. Phil began driving faster.

The Shepards' car raced toward the border. Mike began to foam at the mouth. His skin was pale and sweaty. His breathing became labored.

"We've got an emergency here!" Phil Shepard shouted at the customs officers when the car reached the Mexico-Arizona border. Soon a rescue helicopter was carrying Mike to a hospital.

At the hospital, an emergency room doctor examined Mike. "He has all the signs of a spider bite," she said. After giving Mike a test dose of antivenin, she injected him with a full dose. Within minutes, Mike's condition improved. In three hours, he was released from the hospital, tired but fine.

1. Recognizing Words in Context

Find the word *labored* in the passage. One definition below is a *synonym* for that word; it means the same or almost the same thing. One definition is an *antonym;* it has the opposite or nearly opposite meaning. The other has a completely different meaning. Label the definitions S for *synonym*, A for *antonym*, and D for *different*.

_A_ a. easy

_D_ b. worked

_S_ c. difficult

2. Distinguishing Fact from Opinion

Two of the statements below present *facts*, which can be proved correct. The other statement is an *opinion*, which expresses someone's thoughts or beliefs. Label the statements F for *fact* and O for *opinion*.

_F_ a. Kate saw no mark on Mike's finger.

_F_ b. The doctor gave Mike a test dose of antivenin.

_O_ c. Mike was just overtired.

3. Keeping Events in Order

Two of the statements below describe events that happened at the same time. The other statement describes an event that happened before or after those events. Label them S for *same time,* B for *before,* and A for *after.*

___B___ a. Mike began throwing up.

___S___ b. The car reached the Mexico-Arizona border.

___S___ c. Phil Shepard shouted, "We've got an emergency here!"

4. Making Correct Inferences

Two of the statements below are correct *inferences,* or reasonable guesses. They are based on information in the passage. The other statement is an incorrect, or faulty, inference. Label the statements C for *correct* inference and F for *faulty* inference.

___C___ a. Mike had been bitten by a spider.

___C___ b. The doctor gave Mike a test dose of antivenin to make sure he had no bad reaction to it.

___F___ c. The antivenin would keep Mike safe from future spider bites.

5. Understanding Main Ideas

One of the statements below expresses the main idea of the passage. One statement is too general, or too broad. The other explains only part of the passage; it is too narrow. Label the statements M for *main idea,* B for *too broad,* and N for *too narrow.*

___N___ a. Mike's skin was pale and sweaty, and his breathing was labored.

___B___ b. The bite of some spiders is very dangerous.

___M___ c. After falling ill from a spider bite, Mike Shepard was given a dose of antivenin that saved his life.

Correct Answers, Part A _____

Correct Answers, Part B _____

Total Correct Answers _____

Are you interested in becoming a bird-watcher? One of the first things for a beginner to learn is how to recognize common birds by their shapes. Many parts of a bird's body give clues to its identity. Things to look at are body shape and size. Also look at the length and shape of the tail. The wing shape, bill type, and leg length are still other clues. Where a bird makes its nest provides clues, too.

First, consider the tail. Some tails are forked, like a barn swallow's tail. Some tails are round, like a blue jay's tail, or pointed, like a dove's tail. A mockingbird has a long tail, while the robin's tail is medium length. Some birds, like woodpeckers, use their tails as braces when standing on a tree trunk.

Looking at a bird's beak can help you tell what it is also. Hawks and owls have the large, hooked beaks of meat eaters. The vulture has a less sharply hooked beak. Woodpeckers need long, strong beaks for tapping away at trees all day. The kingfisher's long, pointed beak helps it catch fish more easily. The nighthawk has a very small beak for its size. Its mouth opens wide, however, to scoop in insects while it flies.

Bird-watchers can also use beaks to tell the difference between birds of similar shapes. For instance, the blue jay and the cardinal are shaped alike. When it is dark and you cannot see their color, you can confuse the two birds because of their shapes. The cardinal, however, has a short, thick bill. It is a seedeater. The blue jay is the one with a long, thin beak.

Many birds look alike when they fly. It can be hard to tell them apart by their shapes when they are high in the sky. Geese and cranes may both fly in V-shaped flocks, but other things are different. Cranes fly with their long necks and legs outstretched. Geese also fly with long necks outstretched, but their shorter legs do not go beyond their tail feathers. Herons, which look like cranes, fly with their long necks folded in an S shape.

Keep these hints in mind when you set out to watch birds. See which birds you can recognize and name. Be aware that it takes time to learn all the things that an expert bird-watcher knows. No one becomes an expert overnight.

Reading Time _____

Recalling Facts

1. Blue jays and cardinals have similar
   - ❑ a. body shapes.
   - ❑ b. color.
   - ❑ c. beaks.

   a

2. Birds that have the same shape are
   - ❑ a. blue jays and doves.
   - ❑ b. doves and cardinals.
   - ❑ c. blue jays and cardinals.

   c

3. A barn swallow is noted for its
   - ❑ a. round tail.
   - ❑ b. forked tail.
   - ❑ c. pointed tail.

   b

4. Large, hooked beaks help to identify
   - ❑ a. robins and mockingbirds.
   - ❑ b. geese and herons.
   - ❑ c. owls and hawks.

   c

5. Geese and cranes fly in
   - ❑ a. W-shaped flocks.
   - ❑ b. Y-shaped flocks.
   - ❑ c. V-shaped flocks.

   c

Understanding Ideas

6. The shape of a bird's beak varies with
   - ❑ a. a bird's size.
   - ❑ b. how it is used.
   - ❑ c. a bird's age.

   b

7. The best way to identify a bird at night is most likely by
   - ❑ a. its color.
   - ❑ b. its shape.
   - ❑ c. where it is found.

   b

8. From the article, you can conclude that vultures are
   - ❑ a. small birds.
   - ❑ b. meat eaters.
   - ❑ c. shaped like nighthawks.

   b

9. Something that would probably not help to identify a bird is
   - ❑ a. where it makes its nest.
   - ❑ b. what it eats.
   - ❑ c. who is watching it.

   c

10. You can conclude from the article that all birds
   - ❑ a. have different characteristics.
   - ❑ b. can be easily identified.
   - ❑ c. have similar shapes.

   a

Our neighbor, Mr. Armes, called one morning to say that there was an unusual bird in the marsh. When we got there, the bird was standing hunched over in the water. It was about two feet tall, with a thick body and a short, pointed beak. It was dull brown with white spots on its upper part and white streaks below. None of us had ever seen a bird like it before. As more people arrived, the bird moved off. When some people tried to get close to it, the mystery bird took flight. It flew close to the water and landed where we could still see it.

Mr. Armes had brought a bird book to the marsh. The section on water birds showed two possibilities: an American bittern or a young black-crowned night heron. We decided our mystery bird was a night heron. It didn't have a black neck patch like a bittern has. Its shape was also different from a bittern's. Late that night, we heard the bird's loud kwawk! That told us we were right.

Mr. Armes had taken pictures of the bird. He gave copies to everybody who wanted one. We were glad we had the chance to see the night heron, because it never came back.

1. **Recognizing Words in Context**

   Find the word *pointed* in the passage. One definition below is a *synonym* for that word; it means the same or almost the same thing. One definition is an *antonym;* it has the opposite or nearly opposite meaning. The other has a completely different meaning. Label the definitions S for *synonym,* A for *antonym,* and D for *different.*

   _D_ a. indicated

   _S_ b. sharp

   _A_ c. rounded

2. **Distinguishing Fact from Opinion**

   Two of the statements below present *facts,* which can be proved correct. The other statement is an *opinion,* which expresses someone's thoughts or beliefs. Label the statements F for *fact* and O for *opinion.*

   _F_ a. The bird was about two feet tall, with a thick body and a short, pointed beak.

   _F_ b. An American bittern has a black neck patch.

   _O_ c. Seeing an unusual bird is an exciting event.

3. Keeping Events in Order

Two of the statements below describe events that happened at the same time. The other statement describes an event that happened before or after those events. Label them S for *same time*, B for *before*, and A for *after*.

S   a. More people arrived at the marsh.

A   b. We heard the bird's loud kwawk.

S   c. The bird moved off.

4. Making Correct Inferences

Two of the statements below are correct *inferences*, or reasonable guesses. They are based on information in the passage. The other statement is an incorrect, or faulty, inference. Label the statements C for *correct* inference and F for *faulty* inference.

C   a. Bird-watching was a hobby of Mr. Armes.

C   b. Sometimes the differences between birds are very slight.

F   c. American bittern and black-crowned night heron are different names for the same bird.

5. Understanding Main Ideas

One of the statements below expresses the main idea of the passage. One statement is too general, or too broad. The other explains only part of the passage; it is too narrow. Label the statements M for *main idea*, B for *too broad*, and N for *too narrow*.

B   a. Bird-watching is a hobby enjoyed by many people.

N   b. Mr. Armes called to say that an unusual bird was in the marsh.

M   c. When an unusual bird appears in a marsh, neighbors gather to see and identify it.

Correct Answers, Part A _____

Correct Answers, Part B _____

Total Correct Answers _____

teach

Stories that point out lessons are called fables. Nearly everyone knows the fable about the three little pigs. They leave home to make their fortunes. They build places in which to live. The first little pig makes his house of straw. The second little pig builds his house of sticks. The third little pig works hard to make a house of bricks. It is a good, sturdy house. Along comes a wolf that blows down the houses of straw and sticks. It gobbles up the little pigs. But all its huffing and puffing cannot blow down the house of bricks. The third pig stays safe.

The three little pigs show human characteristics. The story of the little pigs teaches that those who work hard are rewarded. It is just one fable that uses animals to teach a human lesson. Many other fables also use animals to teach lessons. The greatest fable teller, Aesop, told stories that usually featured animals.

In Aesop's "The Lion and the Mouse," the story is about a powerful lion and a tiny mouse. One day, the lion tires of hunting and falls asleep under a tree. Soon a small mouse runs over his face and awakens him. As the angry lion is about to crush the tiny mouse, the mouse begs to live. So the lion lets it go. Some time later, the lion is caught in a hunter's trap. The lion roars with surprise and fury. The mouse hears the roar and races to the trap. It gnaws the ropes and sets the lion free. The powerful lion thanks the mouse and thinks to itself, "Sometimes the weakest can help the strongest."

Aesop's "The Fox and the Stork" shows that a tricky person does not always win. A fox invites a stork to dinner. The fox serves soup in a shallow dish. The poor stork can wet only the end of its long narrow bill in the soup. The sly fox makes false apologies and laps up all the soup. The stork pretends to be satisfied and invites the fox to dinner. When the fox comes a few days later, it finds the food served in a tall jar with a narrow neck. Down in the jar goes the stork's long bill. All the fox can do is lick its chops. This fable may have suggested the old proverb "One who laughs last laughs best."

Reading Time _____

Recalling Facts

1. Fables are stories that
   - ❏ a. describe real events.
   - ❏ b. teach lessons.
   - ❏ c. are about animals.

2. Lessons in Aesop's fables usually feature
   - ❏ a. humans.
   - ❏ b. animals.
   - ❏ c. lions.

3. A well-known fable involves three little
   - ❏ a. pigs.
   - ❏ b. foxes.
   - ❏ c. mice.

4. The mouse in "The Lion and the Mouse" saves the lion from
   - ❏ a. a wolf.
   - ❏ b. a sly fox.
   - ❏ c. a hunter's trap.

5. The fable that shows that a tricky person does not always win is
   - ❏ a. "The Lion and the Mouse."
   - ❏ b. "The Fox and the Stork."
   - ❏ c. "The Three Little Pigs."

Understanding Ideas

6. In fables, animals
   - ❏ a. are only minor characters.
   - ❏ b. act like people.
   - ❏ c. act like real animals.

7. The lessons in fables are directed at
   - ❏ a. animals.
   - ❏ b. people everywhere.
   - ❏ c. people who own animals.

8. If the fables described in the article had human characters, it is likely that
   - ❏ a. the fables would be less enjoyable.
   - ❏ b. the endings would be different.
   - ❏ c. the stories would be shorter.

9. The most likely lesson for a fable is
   - ❏ a. good conquers evil.
   - ❏ b. bigger is better.
   - ❏ c. it is good to be lazy.

10. It is likely that fables are popular because people
   - ❏ a. enjoy stories with unhappy endings.
   - ❏ b. learn to feel guilty about their actions.
   - ❏ c. like to learn lessons in an enjoyable way.

Aesop, Teller of Fables

Aesop became famous as a storyteller when he was living on the island of Samos. He had been a slave there but gained his freedom. Then between 620 and 560 B.C., Aesop went to Lydia. There at the king's court, he met King Croesus. With his intelligence and wit, Aesop quickly pleased the king.

Before long, the king made Aesop an ambassador. He traveled to many places. At Corinth, Aesop told a story that warned the people against mob rule. At Athens, he told the story "The Frogs Desiring a King." This fable warned people that an unknown ruler might be worse than the one they already had.

Aesop's visit to Delphi cost him his life. He was in the city to pay a debt for Croesus. While there, Aesop's sharp tongue made enemies for him. Some of them planted a gold cup from the temple of Apollo in Aesop's baggage. When the cup was found, Aesop was arrested and brought to trial. For once, his storytelling powers failed him. It is said that Aesop appealed to his captors with the fable "The Eagle and the Beetle." The moral of this tale is that the laws of hospitality are not to be broken without punishment. The Delphians broke the laws of hospitality anyway. Aesop was sentenced to death.

1. **Recognizing Words in Context**

   Find the word *planted* in the passage. One definition below is a *synonym* for that word; it means the same or almost the same thing. One definition is an *antonym;* it has the opposite or nearly opposite meaning. The other has a completely different meaning. Label the definitions S for *synonym*, A for *antonym*, and D for *different*.

   ___S___ a. hid

   ___A___ b. removed

   ___D___ c. sowed

2. **Distinguishing Fact from Opinion**

   Two of the statements below present *facts*, which can be proved correct. The other statement is an *opinion*, which expresses someone's thoughts or beliefs. Label the statements F for *fact* and O for *opinion*.

   ___F___ a. Aesop was famous as a teller of fables.

   ___O___ b. The Delphians should have respected Aesop's role as an ambassador.

   ___F___ c. King Croesus used Aesop as an ambassador.

3. Keeping Events in Order

Label the statements below 1, 2, and 3 to show the order in which the events happened.

_1_ a. Aesop received his freedom.

_3_ b. Aesop served as the king's ambassador.

_2_ c. Aesop arrived at the court of Croesus, king of Lydia.

4. Making Correct Inferences

Two of the statements below are correct *inferences,* or reasonable guesses. They are based on information in the passage. The other statement is an incorrect, or faulty, inference. Label the statements C for *correct* inference and F for *faulty* inference.

_C_ a. King Croesus recognized Aesop's intelligence and wit.

_C_ b. Some of Aesop's fables may have kept people from rebelling against their rulers.

_F_ c. The Delphians wanted to start a war with Croesus.

5. Understanding Main Ideas

One of the statements below expresses the main idea of the passage. One statement is too general, or too broad. The other explains only part of the passage; it is too narrow. Label the statements M for *main idea,* B for *too broad,* and N for *too narrow.*

_N_ a. Aesop's enemies planted a gold cup in his baggage.

_M_ b. Aesop, a freed slave and storyteller, became an ambassador of King Croesus.

_B_ c. Aesop was a storyteller.

Correct Answers, Part A _____

Correct Answers, Part B _____

Total Correct Answers _____

Many people don't know how to clean their teeth correctly. Do you always do a good job cleaning your teeth? The goal is to remove all plaque. Plaque is always forming. It coats your teeth. You must do a good cleaning job at least once a day, preferably at night. It takes five to ten minutes to do a good job. To clean your teeth properly, you need a good brush.

Today some people use electric toothbrushes. They are pleasant to use. But you can clean your teeth thoroughly with a regular toothbrush.

To make sure you are doing the job right, you have to follow a few rules. Replace toothbrushes often. A worn-out brush cleans poorly. Its bent bristles can hurt gums.

Use toothpaste or powder. These help clean the teeth. They are refreshing and leave a pleasant taste after brushing. Some toothpaste contains fluoride that helps stop decay. The substance in toothpaste called abrasives helps clean teeth but may also wear away tooth enamel. Toothpastes vary in the amount of abrasives they contain. Check with your dentist about the brand you use. Baking soda or a mixture of baking soda and salt can clean teeth well. They save you money, too.

The use of dental floss helps remove food from places your toothbrush cannot reach. If you have not been using floss, you may find flossing difficult to do at first. But flossing gets easier with daily practice. It is a good idea to check with your dentist to be sure that you are flossing properly. When using floss, be careful not to cut into the gums.

Plaque causes tooth decay. A good light and a mirror will show up plaque if you have any. Your drugstore sells wafers or liquids that you can use for this same purpose. These stain plaque red or blue so that you can see it. By staining the plaque after brushing and flossing, you can see which areas you may have missed. Clean these areas again.

There are other aids that can be used to clean between teeth. Your drugstore sells special toothpicks that can be used to scrape away plaque. Water sprays are available, too. These are used to remove loose bits of food from between teeth. These should be used with care to avoid damaging the gums. None of these aids replaces the toothbrush and floss for removing plaque.

Reading Time _____

Recalling Facts

1. The goal in cleaning your teeth is to
   - ❏ a. remove plaque.
   - ❏ b. scrape your gums.
   - ❏ c. flush your teeth with water.

2. A chemical that helps stop tooth decay is called
   - ❏ a. baking soda.
   - ❏ b. fluoride.
   - ❏ c. floss.

3. To clean where toothbrushes cannot reach, use
   - ❏ a. mouthwash.
   - ❏ b. dental floss.
   - ❏ c. plaque stains.

4. You can use a tablet or liquid to stain areas where you have
   - ❏ a. tooth decay.
   - ❏ b. gum problems.
   - ❏ c. plaque on your teeth.

5. Abrasives in toothpaste may
   - ❏ a. wear away tooth enamel.
   - ❏ b. cause cavities.
   - ❏ c. coat your teeth.

Understanding Ideas

6. Electric toothbrushes
   - ❏ a. clean better than regular toothbrushes.
   - ❏ b. should be used instead of floss.
   - ❏ c. are effective for cleaning teeth.

7. Plaque should be removed
   - ❏ a. continually.
   - ❏ b. by your dentist.
   - ❏ c. only once.

8. Using baking soda to clean your teeth is probably
   - ❏ a. better than using toothpaste.
   - ❏ b. less expensive than toothpaste.
   - ❏ c. not as effective as using tooth-paste.

9. The article suggests that brushing your teeth
   - ❏ a. is the best way to clean them properly.
   - ❏ b. should be combined with flossing to clean them properly.
   - ❏ c. is not as effective as using dental floss.

10. You can conclude from the article that keeping teeth clean
    - ❏ a. will avoid decay.
    - ❏ b. helps to avoid tooth and gum problems.
    - ❏ c. is an impossible job.

The Nylon Toothbrush

Du Pont scientists discovered nylon in the 1930s. At the time, they did not know that nylon would change the toothbrush industry. Toothbrushes had long been made with hog-hair bristles. Du Pont decided to make brushes with nylon bristles instead. Nylon had many advantages. Nylon was tough and stiff. It tended to keep its shape. Moisture could not soak into it. This discouraged the growth of bacteria.

Du Pont introduced the first nylon-bristle toothbrush in 1938. It was named Dr. West's Miracle Tuft Toothbrush. Ads for the new brush pointed out that hog-hair bristles often pulled free of the brush. When they did, they could get stuck between teeth. The nylon bristles in the new toothbrush were fastened better. They were not likely to pull free.

Users of the new toothbrush found, however, that nylon bristles had a disadvantage. They were hard on gums. Because of this, dentists did not recommend the new toothbrushes. Du Pont worked to improve the brushes. By the early 1950s, the company perfected a softer nylon that did not tear gums.

Nylon toothbrushes became widely used. People who used them improved their dental hygiene. They also spared hogs around the world from having their bristles pulled out. The year before nylon-bristle toothbrushes were introduced, the United States imported 1.5 million pounds of hog bristles!

1. Recognizing Words in Context

Find the word *used* in the passage. One definition below is a *synonym* for that word; it means the same or almost the same thing. One definition is an *antonym;* it has the opposite or nearly opposite meaning. The other has a completely different meaning. Label the definitions S for *synonym,* A for *antonym,* and D for *different.*

A a. discarded
D b. secondhand
S c. utilized

2. Distinguishing Fact from Opinion

Two of the statements below present *facts,* which can be proved correct. The other statement is an *opinion,* which expresses someone's thoughts or beliefs. Label the statements F for *fact* and O for *opinion.*

F a. Du Pont chemists discovered nylon in the 1930s.
F b. Before nylon, toothbrush bristles were made of hog hair.
O c. People should have given up hog-hair toothbrushes for nylon-bristle ones.

3. Keeping Events in Order

Label the statements below 1, 2, and 3 to show the order in which the events happened.

___2___ a. Nylon toothbrush bristles tore gum tissue.

___1___ b. Nylon was discovered by Du Pont chemists.

___3___ c. Du Pont developed a softer kind of nylon.

4. Making Correct Inferences

Two of the statements below are correct *inferences*, or reasonable guesses. They are based on information in the passage. The other statement is an incorrect, or faulty, inference. Label the statements C for *correct* inference and F for *faulty* inference.

___F___ a. After 1938, all toothbrush bristles were made of nylon.

___C___ b. Nylon bristles were a major improvement over hog-hair bristles.

___C___ c. After softer nylon bristles were developed, dentists recommended nylon-bristle toothbrushes to their patients.

5. Understanding Main Ideas

One of the statements below expresses the main idea of the passage. One statement is too general, or too broad. The other explains only part of the passage; it is too narrow. Label the statements M for *main idea*, B for *too broad*, and N for *too narrow*.

___B___ a. Toothbrushes have improved.

___N___ b. Nylon was tough, stiff, and tended to keep its shape.

___M___ c. The discovery of nylon in the 1930s changed the way toothbrushes were made.

Correct Answers, Part A _____

Correct Answers, Part B _____

Total Correct Answers _____

To survive, animals learn how to adjust to changes in their world. Some have learned how to live through cold winters when food is in short supply. Their secret is a winter sleep called hibernation. When temperatures drop, these animals go to sleep.

The best-known hibernator is the bear. All bears can hibernate. But mainly it is those that live in colder climates that do.

Before bears settle down for a long winter sleep, they stuff themselves with food. Bears eat many kinds of food including fish. But one of their favorite foods is honey. They will do almost anything to get it. They also like berries. Berries help a bear put on the extra fat it needs for its long winter sleep. In the late summer and early fall, ripe berries are plentiful. Hungry bears eat as many berries as they can find. Some bears may even travel as much as a hundred miles (160 kilometers) to feast on berries.

It is true that bears hibernate during the winter because food is scarce. Yet, they have another reason to take to the den during the cold months. This is when their cubs are born. Bear cubs are usually born two to a litter. At birth, they are very tiny compared to their mother. She may weigh as much as 600 to 800 pounds (270 to 360 kilograms). Her cubs may weigh less than a pound (one-half kilogram) apiece. The cubs are blind and helpless during the first few weeks after birth. In this state, they could never survive the harsh cold. The winter den keeps the cubs safe and warm.

Bears' winter dens vary with the kind of bear that uses them and the climate of the area. The dens of smaller bears may be little more than a hollow stump. Some dens are just holes dug in a riverbank. Larger bears, however, need bigger dens. Grizzlies, for example, dig out a den that is 10 to 12 feet (3 to 3.5 meters) deep. They bed it down with leaves. Then they seal it with earth and stones. Some bears in Yellowstone National Park even enjoy steam-heated caves among the hot springs. Black bears often build a den under a thick pile of logs. Or they may choose the roots of an upturned tree and let the heavy winter snows provide a good roof. Hibernating keeps bears safe and sound.

Reading Time _____

Recalling Facts

1. Animals hibernate because
   - ❏ a. they don't like cold weather.
   - ❏ b. food is scarce.
   - ❏ c. they need rest.

   b

2. Berries are ripe during
   - ❏ a. early fall.
   - ❏ b. the late winter.
   - ❏ c. early summer.

   a

3. Bears usually give birth to
   - ❏ a. one cub.
   - ❏ b. two cubs.
   - ❏ c. three cubs.

   b

4. Bears' dens vary with the kind of bear and the
   - ❏ a. climate.
   - ❏ b. time of year.
   - ❏ c. number of cubs that are born.

   a

5. Black bears often build dens in
   - ❏ a. hollow stumps.
   - ❏ b. thick piles of logs.
   - ❏ c. earth and stones.

   b

Understanding Ideas

6. You can conclude from the article that in cold climates
   - ❏ a. all animals hibernate.
   - ❏ b. only bears hibernate.
   - ❏ c. some animals hibernate.

   C

7. Hibernation is one way that animals have learned to
   - ❏ a. find needed food.
   - ❏ b. sleep better.
   - ❏ c. adjust to their surroundings.

   C

8. If bears did not hibernate, their cubs would most likely
   - ❏ a. starve.
   - ❏ b. die from the cold.
   - ❏ c. get lost.

   b

9. Bears that live in warm climates
   - ❏ a. hibernate during the summer.
   - ❏ b. travel north to hibernate.
   - ❏ c. do not need to hibernate.

   C

10. You can conclude from the article that bears
    - ❏ a. are plant eaters.
    - ❏ b. are meat eaters.
    - ❏ c. eat meat and plants.

    C

6 B   Teaching a Cub to Hibernate

On his rounds, a Montana forest ranger found an orphaned bear cub. It was thin and weak. During their first year, cubs depend on their mother to teach them how to find food so that they will be fat enough to get through the winter. She also teaches them how to dig a den in which to hibernate. If anything happens to their mother, cubs often die.

The ranger took the cub to a shelter run by Montana's Fish, Wildlife, and Parks Department (FWPD). There shelter workers cared for the cub. They fed it the same kinds of berries, grasses, and fruits its mother would have supplied. The cub slept outdoors in a crate filled with hay. As winter approached, the workers cut back on the cub's food. It began to get sleepy.

Shelter workers dug a den in the woods. They filled the den with familiar-smelling hay from the cub's crate. They tranquilized the cub, fitted it with a radio collar, and carried it to the den on a snowmobile. There they put the sleeping cub to bed for the winter. They hoped that the cub would remember what to do when it woke up in the spring.

Since 1988, the FWPD has rescued more than fifty cubs. Most have survived. They have gone on to find food on their own and den by themselves the next winter.

1. Recognizing Words in Context

Find the word *fat* in the passage. One definition below is a *synonym* for that word; it means the same or almost the same thing. One definition is an *antonym;* it has the opposite or nearly opposite meaning. The other has a completely different meaning. Label the definitions S for *synonym*, A for *antonym*, and D for *different*.

_A_ a. thin

_D_ b. grease

_S_ c. plump

2. Distinguishing Fact from Opinion

Two of the statements below present *facts*, which can be proved correct. The other statement is an *opinion*, which expresses someone's thoughts or beliefs. Label the statements F for *fact* and O for *opinion*.

_O_ a. Rescuing bear cubs is a wonderful thing to do.

_F_ b. Since 1988, the FWPD has rescued more than fifty cubs.

_F_ c. Montana's Fish, Wildlife, and Parks Department has a program to save orphaned bear cubs.

35

3. Keeping Events in Order

Label the statements below 1, 2, and 3 to show the order in which the events happened.

_2_   a. Workers fed the cub berries, grasses, and fruit.

_3_   b. The cub was left in a den dug by shelter workers.

_1_   c. A ranger brought an orphaned bear cub to the FWPD shelter.

4. Making Correct Inferences

Two of the statements below are correct *inferences,* or reasonable guesses. They are based on information in the passage. The other statement is an incorrect, or faulty, inference. Label the statements C for *correct* inference and F for *faulty* inference.

_C_   a. The relationship between a mother bear and her cub is important to the cub's survival.

_F_   b. Most orphaned bear cubs can survive without human help.

_C_   c. Montana's program saves cubs that would otherwise die.

5. Understanding Main Ideas

One of the statements below expresses the main idea of the passage. One statement is too general, or too broad. The other explains only part of the passage; it is too narrow. Label the statements M for *main idea,* B for *too broad,* and N for *too narrow.*

_M_   a. The Montana FWPD saves orphaned bear cubs by feeding them natural foods and providing a den for them.

_N_   b. Workers tranquilized the cub and took it to the den on a snowmobile.

_B_   c. Bears hibernate during the winter.

Correct Answers, Part A _____

Correct Answers, Part B _____

Total Correct Answers _____

Death on the Mississippi

It was April of 1865. Floodwaters were overflowing the banks of the Mississippi. But no one paid much attention to the tricks of the river. The Civil War had ended at last, and there was peace in the land. A bitterness, sadness, and weariness hung heavily over the soldiers who had fought. They were sick of war and wanted to go home.

At Vicksburg, thousands of Union soldiers were gathered. These soldiers had fought for the North and were anxious to go home. The most anxious were those who had just been freed from southern prison camps. They were pale and weak and could only think of home. They badly needed rest and care and good food. And they needed to be back with their families.

When the steamboat *Sultana* made a landing at Vicksburg, the soldiers rushed to get aboard. They crowded into the hull. They packed the cabins and even the pilothouse. Still they came until the steamer could hold no more. There were about 2,300 persons on a boat meant to carry 376.

The *Sultana's* captain was worried. He had had trouble with the boilers. The river's current was unusually strong. But the boat eased away from the wharf and went puffing upstream. Forty-eight hours later, the ship put in at Memphis.

A number of soldiers went ashore to see the sights. Some of them did not get back by sailing time. They found that the boat had left without them.

Through the night, the *Sultana* pushed on. Her big paddle wheels beat against the strong current. Midnight passed, and then one o'clock. Around two in the morning, the boat swung around a bend in the dark river. Suddenly, it happened.

The boilers exploded with a tremendous crash. Flames roared up into the dark sky. Hundreds of soldiers were blown into the river. Red-hot coals, twisted machinery, bits and pieces of wood, and furniture flew through the air. The boat caught fire. The soldiers still aboard had to leap into the icy-cold water or be burned alive.

Many could not swim. Those who could swim were too weak from prison to last for very long.

In the first light of dawn, rescue ships came steaming up from Memphis. They picked up hundreds of survivors, but they were still too late. About 1700 soldiers were dead. They died in one of the worst steamboat accidents in United States history.

Reading Time _____

Recalling Facts

1. Soldiers who fought for the Union in the Civil War were
   - ☑ a. northern soldiers.
   - ❏ b. southern soldiers.
   - ❏ c. mostly farmers.

2. In April 1865, the Civil War
   - ❏ a. started.
   - ❏ b. expanded.
   - ☑ c. ended.

3. The *Sultana* was a
   - ❏ a. rescue boat.
   - ❏ b. pilot house.
   - ☑ c. steamboat.

4. Disaster occurred aboard the *Sultana* when the
   - ❏ a. boat hit a rock.
   - ❏ b. boilers exploded.
   - ❏ c. captain got lost.

5. Many aboard the *Sultana* were
   - ❏ a. escaped prisoners.
   - ☑ b. released prisoners.
   - ❏ c. prisoners being sent to a new prison.

Understanding Ideas

6. A likely cause of the *Sultana* accident was
   - ☑ a. excess weight.
   - ❏ b. bad weather.
   - ❏ c. the Civil War.

7. You can conclude from the article that fire resulted from
   - ❏ a. enemy fire.
   - ❏ b. a fire built for warmth.
   - ☑ c. flames used to heat water to provide steam.

8. The article suggests that more people would have survived the *Sultana* accident if
   - ❏ a. the war had ended sooner.
   - ☑ b. the soldiers had not been weakened by prison.
   - ❏ c. more rescue ships had arrived.

9. You can conclude that the soldiers who missed the boat in Memphis
   - ☑ a. were very lucky.
   - ❏ b. would probably have survived the accident.
   - ❏ c. did so on purpose.

10. The article suggests that steamboats were
    - ❏ a. very dangerous.
    - ☑ b. a common means of travel.
    - ❏ c. often overcrowded.

It had been raining for months, Cora Lee Dwight thought. She couldn't remember when she had last seen the sun. The Mississippi River was swollen with water. Just that morning she was amazed to see a sternwheeler paddle by in full view. Its smokestacks towered high above the levee. Under normal conditions, the steamboat would have been hidden behind the levee's wall.

People had begun to worry about flooding. "Won't the levee hold the river, Dad?" Cora Lee asked her father.

"The levee's only a wall of earth, Cora Lee," her father answered. "If the river gets high enough, the levee won't hold."

Neither of them knew that upstream, the waters of the Mississippi had broken through the levee with a mighty roar. Where farmland had once been, there was a vast sea of water. It was 80 miles (129 km) wide and 18 feet (5.5 m) deep in places.

Within days, the flood reached Cora Lee's hometown. She helped her parents pile things on top of tables to keep them safe. They were safe only until the floodwater reached that high. It went higher yet. Cora Lee watched in tears from a second-story window as her piano floated out the front door.

1. **Recognizing Words in Context**

Find the word *hold* in the passage. One definition below is a *synonym* for that word; it means the same or almost the same thing. One definition is an *antonym*; it has the opposite or nearly opposite meaning. The other has a completely different meaning. Label the definitions S for *synonym*, A for *antonym*, and D for *different*.

  D   a. stay strong

  S   b. grasp

  A   c. weaken

2. **Distinguishing Fact from Opinion**

Two of the statements below present *facts*, which can be proved correct. The other statement is an *opinion*, which expresses someone's thoughts or beliefs. Label the statements F for *fact* and O for *opinion*.

  F   a. A vast sea of water covered what had been farmland.

  F   b. The Mississippi River broke through the levee.

  O   c. It seemed as if it had been raining for months.

39

3. Keeping Events in Order

Two of the statements below describe events that happened at the same time. The other statement describes an event that happened before or after those events. Label them S for *same time,* B for *before,* and A for *after.*

_____ a. Cora Lee watched from an upstairs window.

_____ b. Cora Lee's piano floated out the door of the house.

_____ c. The floodwater reached Cora Lee's hometown.

4. Making Correct Inferences

Two of the statements below are correct *inferences,* or reasonable guesses. They are based on information in the passage. The other statement is an incorrect, or faulty, inference. Label the statements C for *correct* inference and F for *faulty* inference.

_____ a. Heavy rain over a long period of time had caused the river to flood.

_____ b. People had believed the levee would protect them from floods.

_____ c. There is still a vast sea of water covering farmland in the Mississippi River valley.

5. Understanding Main Ideas

One of the statements below expresses the main idea of the passage. One statement is too general, or too broad. The other explains only part of the passage; it is too narrow. Label the statements M for *main idea,* B for *too broad,* and N for *too narrow.*

_____ a. Under normal conditions, the steamboat would have been hidden behind the levee wall.

_____ b. The Mississippi River and its tributaries drain some 40 percent of the United States.

_____ c. Swollen with rainwater, the Mississippi River bursts through a levee and floods farmland along its banks.

Correct Answers, Part A _____

Correct Answers, Part B _____

Total Correct Answers _____

Leaving a Fire

The time to plan for a fire emergency is before it happens. This is when everyone is calm and clear thinking. This is when decisions about safe escape routes can be discussed and made. Have a family meeting. Don't delay. It's too late to plan after a fire starts.

Knowing ahead of time how to get out during a fire can save lives. The best way out in a fire is the route you use to go in and out every day. Yet, in a fire this route may be blocked. Be sure to plan other escape routes.

Take each person to his or her room and describe what to do in case of fire. Give everyone a job. Older children should take care of younger ones. Plans may have to be made for anyone who cannot escape without help. Adults who can't walk should sleep on the first floor. Small children should sleep near older persons who can help them. Only healthy, able persons should sleep in hard-to-reach attics or basements.

Practice your escape plan at night when it is dark. This will help you decide whether your plan will work well. If it does not, then revise your plan. For instance, make sure that a child can actually open the window he or she is supposed to use for escape. Teach children to close their bedroom doors. Tell them to wait by an open window until someone can reach them from outside. Children should be taught that if an adult cannot be awakened, the children must leave by themselves. Choose a meeting place outside. This way you can tell whether everyone is safely out of the building. Know where nearby telephones or fire alarm boxes are found.

If you live in an apartment, learn where the fire alarm is in the building. Your family should know what the fire alarm bell sounds like. They should know what to do when they hear it. Try to get the other families together to have fire drills. Write down the telephone number of the fire department. Tape the number to each phone. Don't forget to let the baby-sitter in on your plans. Tell your baby-sitter what to do in case of fire.

Early warning is the key to a safe escape from a fire. It has been shown time and time again that a family can escape when warned early enough.

Reading Time _____

Recalling Facts

1. The time to plan for a fire emergency is
   - ❏ a. before one happens.
   - ❏ b. during the emergency.
   - ❏ c. after an emergency happens.

2. The best way out in a fire is
   - ❏ a. a window.
   - ❏ b. jumping from the roof.
   - ❏ c. the route you use every day.

3. The key to a safe escape from a fire is
   - ❏ a. practice.
   - ❏ b. early warning.
   - ❏ c. the fire department.

4. It is a good idea to practice an escape plan
   - ❏ a. when it is dark.
   - ❏ b. every day.
   - ❏ c. early in the morning.

5. After escaping from a fire, you should
   - ❏ a. gather at an agreed-upon place.
   - ❏ b. call an ambulance.
   - ❏ c. run back into the building.

Understanding Ideas

6. You can conclude from the article that in a fire emergency,
   - ❏ a. it is important to move slowly.
   - ❏ b. every second counts.
   - ❏ c. everyone needs help.

7. It is likely that people involved in a fire emergency will be
   - ❏ a. cowardly.
   - ❏ b. panicky.
   - ❏ c. calm.

8. It is important to plan a variety of escape routes because
   - ❏ a. plans should be complicated.
   - ❏ b. it is easy to get lost in a fire.
   - ❏ c. one or more routes may be blocked by fire.

9. You can conclude that the longer a family takes to escape, the
   - ❏ a. more damage a fire will cause.
   - ❏ b. more likely they are to escape safely.
   - ❏ c. less likely they are to escape safely.

10. You can conclude that escape from fire is
    - ❏ a. highly unlikely.
    - ❏ b. impossible unless a plan is followed.
    - ❏ c. possible.

Sherry woke with a start. What had awakened her? A strong stench made her cough. That was it! She was smelling smoke!

Sherry jumped from her bed. She knew exactly what to do. Her family had prepared a fire escape plan and had conducted several fire drills. Sherry opened the window to her bedroom and let down the rope ladder attached to the inside of the windowsill. Then she woke up her sister Margie, who shared her room. Without opening her bedroom door, Sherry began yelling "Fire!" to wake up her parents. Just as she did, she heard the wail of the smoke detectors in the hall. That would wake them up!

Sherry led Margie to the window. She stepped over the sill and onto the ladder. Then she helped Margie do the same. Step by slow step, the two girls climbed down the ladder. When they were safe, they waited on the sidewalk.

In the distance, Sherry and Margie heard the wail of sirens. A neighbor must have called the fire department. Just as Sherry was beginning to worry, her parents stumbled out of the house. The four of them hugged each other in relief. "Well done, girls!" Sherry's dad said. "Our practice really paid off."

1. **Recognizing Words in Context**

   Find the word *start* in the passage. One definition below is a *synonym* for that word; it means the same or almost the same thing. One definition is an *antonym*; it has the opposite or nearly opposite meaning. The other has a completely different meaning. Label the definitions S for *synonym*, A for *antonym*, and D for *different*.

   __S__ a. jerk

   __A__ b. smoothly

   __D__ c. begin

2. **Distinguishing Fact from Opinion**

   Two of the statements below present *facts*, which can be proved correct. The other statement is an *opinion*, which expresses someone's thoughts or beliefs. Label the statements F for *fact* and O for *opinion*.

   __F__ a. The family had practiced what to do in the event of a fire.

   __F__ b. The smell of smoke awakened Sherry.

   __O__ c. The family was wise to have practiced what each member should do if there were a fire.

3. Keeping Events in Order

Label the statements below 1, 2, and 3 to show the order in which the events happened.

___1___ a. Sherry opened her bedroom window.

___3___ b. Sherry began yelling "Fire!"

___2___ c. Sherry woke up her sister Margie.

4. Making Correct Inferences

Two of the statements below are correct *inferences*, or reasonable guesses. They are based on information in the passage. The other statement is an incorrect, or faulty, inference. Label the statements C for *correct* inference and F for *faulty* inference.

___C___ a. Sherry correctly remembered the steps she should take in case of fire.

___F___ b. Sherry thought only of herself and her sister, not of her parents.

___C___ c. Sherry's calm thinking saved her and her sister from the fire.

5. Understanding Main Ideas

One of the statements below expresses the main idea of the passage. One statement is too general, or too broad. The other explains only part of the passage; it is too narrow. Label the statements M for *main idea*, B for *too broad*, and N for *too narrow*.

___M___ a. Because her family had practiced what to do in case of fire, a young girl named Sherry saves her sister and herself.

___B___ b. The time to plan for a fire emergency is before it happens.

___N___ c. Sherry opened her bedroom window and let down a rope ladder attached to the inside of the windowsill.

Correct Answers, Part A _____

Correct Answers, Part B _____

Total Correct Answers _____

Backpacking

Countless people today enjoy the pleasures and benefits of mountain hiking. Backpacking offers freedom found in no other type of wilderness travel. However, you must know what to expect when you hike off into the wilderness. There will be no piped water or shelters to use. There will be no tables to eat from and no grills to hold your pots and pans. There will be few trail signs to guide you. You must know how to follow a map. You will be on your own.

Still, there are countless places you can go. Try an overnight trip to a mountain or stream. Follow an unmarked trail that seems inviting. A trial run will help tone up muscles and show up mistakes in plans. During a short trip, you will not suffer too badly if something has been left at home.

Experienced backpackers pride themselves on being able to travel light. With many, weight saving is a game. Some cut towels in half and saw the handles off toothbrushes to save ounces. They measure out just the right amount of food needed and put it in plastic bags. Plastic bags are lighter than cardboard. There are dozens of tricks to save ounces (grams) that add up to pounds (kilograms).

Footwear is an important thing to keep in mind. Sneakers are cool and cheap. For youngsters who are growing, the heavy-soled, ankle-high sneaker is best. Rubber is good where the going is wet. Hikers in swamps and bogs prefer the shoepac above anything else. However, leather is the most popular shoe material for all-around hiking. It wears well and is soft. It can be waterproofed to shed snow and rain.

Leather soles on boots are slippery. Most hikers use rubber or cord soles. When the soles wear out, thick rubber lug soles can be put on. These grip the rocks well.

Hiking boots should fit comfortably over two pairs of socks, one thin and one thick. They should protect the ankles and support the foot. They have to withstand long distances, sometimes on rocks and roots. Be sure that boots are well broken in before the trip. A mountain trail is no place to break in a new pair of boots. Ski boots are for skiing and cowboy boots are for horseback riding. Footwear with eyelets and lacing has proved best for hiking. A wise hiker always brings an extra pair of laces.

Reading Time _____

Recalling Facts

1. When packing for a hike, backpackers try to
   - ❏ a. add ounces.
   - ❏ b. stock extra supplies.
   - ❏ c. save weight.

2. The most popular shoes for all-around hiking are made of
   - ❏ a. rubber.
   - ❏ b. light fabric.
   - ❏ c. leather.

3. Hikers should wear
   - ❏ a. new boots.
   - ❏ b. comfortable boots.
   - ❏ c. boots with leather soles.

4. In the wilderness, most hiking trails
   - ❏ a. are unmarked.
   - ❏ b. follow natural streams.
   - ❏ c. are well marked.

5. Mistakes in plans should be corrected
   - ❏ a. on a map.
   - ❏ b. after a trial run.
   - ❏ c. during a long hike.

Understanding Ideas

6. Backpackers should most likely plan on
   - ❏ a. bringing their own sleeping shelters.
   - ❏ b. sleeping outside.
   - ❏ c. sleeping in cabins along the way.

7. The article suggests that backpacking
   - ❏ a. can be dangerous.
   - ❏ b. is challenging.
   - ❏ c. requires little planning.

8. Backpacking is probably not an activity for
   - ❏ a. youngsters.
   - ❏ b. people who like adventure.
   - ❏ c. people who are out of shape.

9. You can conclude from the article that it is important for backpackers to
   - ❏ a. wear the proper clothing.
   - ❏ b. wear several layers of clothing.
   - ❏ c. carry a heavy jacket.

10. When hiking in the wilderness, you should have the goal to
    - ❏ a. know exactly where you are at all times.
    - ❏ b. enjoy the freedom of wilderness travel.
    - ❏ c. follow marked trails.

Don't Ask

When Kim showed up for their hike, Anita was surprised. Kim had on a T-shirt, shorts, and leather-sole shoes. Kim was definitely not dressed for hiking. Anita was wearing a warm sweatshirt, jeans, and hiking boots. Anita's brother was waiting impatiently in the car to drive them to the mountain. It was too late to tell Kim to go home and change into more appropriate clothing. Anita grabbed a jacket, and they ran to the car.

As soon as they started hiking, Anita realized she had made a mistake. The trail was rough. Prickly vines scratched Kim's legs. Her feet slipped on loose stones. As they got higher up the mountain, Kim started to shiver. Anita gave her the jacket, but Kim was still cold. They ate the lunch they had brought, but it didn't help Kim. She walked more and more slowly.

Although they were nowhere near the top, Anita decided to turn around. Going down was even harder. Kim's smooth-soled shoes slipped on the rocks, and she fell. She was almost too tired to pick herself up.

Anita was worried. Fortunately, some other hikers came along and offered to help Kim get down the mountain. They went the rest of the way together. Anita's brother was waiting for them at the base of the trail. "What took you so long?" he asked.

"Don't ask!" Anita said.

1. Recognizing Words in Context

Find the word *harder* in the passage. One definition below is a *synonym* for that word; it means the same or almost the same thing. One definition is an *antonym;* it has the opposite or nearly opposite meaning. The other has a completely different meaning. Label the definitions S for *synonym*, A for *antonym*, and D for *different*.

___D___ a. firmer

___A___ b. easier

___S___ c. more difficult

2. Distinguishing Fact from Opinion

Two of the statements below present *facts*, which can be proved correct. The other statement is an *opinion*, which expresses someone's thoughts or beliefs. Label the statements F for *fact* and O for *opinion*.

___F___ a. Anita wore a sweatshirt, jeans, and hiking boots.

___O___ b. Anita should not have let Kim hike the way she was dressed.

___F___ c. Prickly vines scratched Kim's legs.

47

3. Keeping Events in Order

Two of the statements below describe events that happened at the same time. The other statement describes an event that happened before or after those events. Label them S for *same time,* B for *before,* and A for *after.*

_B_ a. Kim showed up wearing a T-shirt, shorts, and leather-sole shoes.

_S_ b. The two girls started hiking up the mountain.

_A_ c. Anita realized she had made a mistake.

4. Making Correct Inferences

Two of the statements below are correct *inferences,* or reasonable guesses. They are based on information in the passage. The other statement is an incorrect, or faulty, inference. Label the statements C for *correct* inference and F for *faulty* inference.

_____ a. The problems on the trail were all Kim's fault.

_____ b. Anita was an experienced hiker.

_____ c. Kim did not know how to dress for hiking up a mountain.

5. Understanding Main Ideas

One of the statements below expresses the main idea of the passage. One statement is too general, or too broad. The other explains only part of the passage; it is too narrow. Label the statements M for *main idea,* B for *too broad,* and N for *too narrow.*

_____ a. Countless people today enjoy the pleasures of mountain hiking.

_____ b. Kim's smooth-soled shoes slipped on the rocks, and she fell.

_____ c. Two girls on a hike have a series of problems because one of them is not properly dressed for the conditions.

Correct Answers, Part A _____

Correct Answers, Part B _____

Total Correct Answers _____

Why are people tracking the wild goose? Why would anyone want to? There is one kind of wild goose called the Emperor Goose. It is spied upon, followed, and watched. Every move that it makes is noticed and carefully written down. But don't feel sorry for the Emperor Goose. It's all for the goose's own good.

Little is known about this goose. It is a lovely and rare North American waterfowl. Because this goose is so rare, researchers want to be sure that it will survive. To do this, they have to know and understand its habits.

The known nesting place of the Emperor Goose is small. It is found in a semiwild part of the state of Alaska. The land around Kokechik Bay seems to attract the bird. The streams of the Yukon delta empty into the bay. These same streams carry pollution to the nesting sites, especially after a storm. The researchers want to learn how human acts affect the birds. First, however, people must know something about the goose itself.

To find answers to questions, researchers have set up camps near the breeding grounds. After locating and studying the nests, scientists have learned many things. For example, they now know how the female guards her nest. She presses close to the ground. She stretches her neck out and remains quite still. In this way, she looks like a piece of driftwood. And who would bother with a piece of driftwood?

Scientists have also learned that after the Emperor Geese mate, they stay together. While the female sits on the eggs, the male stands or feeds nearby. At times, the male may wander off a little way. He is sure to come back quickly if the female is disturbed.

When the eggs hatch, the young geese are a dark gray color. After two weeks, the dark gray turns to a light gray. When the goslings reach the fledgling stage, they take on a blue tone. The adult goose can be recognized by the whiteness of its head and the back of its neck. This white contrasts with the black of its throat. Its silver-gray feathers and its bright yellow-orange feet make this bird one of the most colorful geese.

Scientists need to know a lot more about the Emperor Goose. The researchers in Alaska hope to add to their knowledge in order to protect this amazing bird.

Reading Time _____

Recalling Facts

1. The Emperor Goose is found in
   - ❑ a. Australia.
   - ❑ b. South America.
   - ❑ c. North America.

2. To study the birds, scientists
   - ❑ a. read books about them.
   - ❑ b. set up camps near the breeding grounds.
   - ❑ c. place them in zoos.

3. After the Emperor Geese mate,
   - ❑ a. the male flies away.
   - ❑ b. the female wanders off.
   - ❑ c. they stay together.

4. Goslings take on a blue tone
   - ❑ a. when they get cold.
   - ❑ b. after they hatch.
   - ❑ c. when they reach the fledgling stage.

5. The head of the adult goose
   - ❑ a. makes it very colorful.
   - ❑ b. is white in color.
   - ❑ c. matches its yellow-orange feet.

Understanding Ideas

6. The article suggests that the Emperor Goose
   - ❑ a. is threatened by pollution.
   - ❑ b. will soon become extinct.
   - ❑ c. is too rare to survive.

7. You can conclude from the article that Emperor Geese prefer
   - ❑ a. a warm climate.
   - ❑ b. a cool climate.
   - ❑ c. a stormy environment.

8. You can conclude that the Emperor Goose protects its nest by
   - ❑ a. resembling its surroundings.
   - ❑ b. choosing small nesting sites.
   - ❑ c. changing colors.

9. Probably the best way to study a wild creature is to
   - ❑ a. capture it.
   - ❑ b. look at photographs.
   - ❑ c. enter its habitat.

10. You can conclude that the more that is learned about the Emperor Goose,
    - ❑ a. the more likely it is to survive.
    - ❑ b. the faster it will multiply.
    - ❑ c. the more geese scientists can find.

Gathering Geese

Vernon Byrd is a biologist with the U.S. Fish and Wildlife Service (FWS) in Alaska. He was assigned the job of rounding up rare and endangered Aleutian Canada geese. He was supposed to move them to other islands. The geese lived only on the rocky island of Buldir, which is at the western tip of Alaska. Byrd took a group of FWS workers to the island during August. At that time, the geese were growing new feathers and could not fly. The workers chased the geese with nets, but the shy geese ran faster. They hid in the tall grass. After three weeks on the cold, windy, rainy island, the unhappy workers had caught only 120 geese.

Then Byrd heard about another FWS worker who was using border collies to herd geese. He asked whether the dogs could work on Buldir. He and the dogs' owner worried that the dogs might get hurt on the wet rocks. The next August, however, they decided to see how the dogs would do.

The border collies went to work eagerly. In just four days, they rounded up 143 geese. Workers could then pick the geese up easily. The project was a great success. Now the FWS is thinking of other ways to use trained dogs in their work to save endangered species.

1. Recognizing Words in Context

Find the word *rare* in the passage. One definition below is a *synonym* for that word; it means the same or almost the same thing. One definition is an *antonym*; it has the opposite or nearly opposite meaning. The other has a completely different meaning. Label the definitions S for *synonym*, A for *antonym*, and D for *different*.

_____ a. common

_____ b. unusual

_____ c. excellent

2. Distinguishing Fact from Opinion

Two of the statements below present *facts*, which can be proved correct. The other statement is an *opinion*, which expresses someone's thoughts or beliefs. Label the statements F for *fact* and O for *opinion*.

_____ a. The Fish and Wildlife Service should have left the geese alone.

_____ b. Buldir is an island at the western tip of Alaska.

_____ c. The Fish and Wildlife Service workers captured only 120 geese in three weeks.

3. Keeping Events in Order

Label the statements below 1, 2, and 3 to show the order in which the events happened.

_____ a. The dogs captured 143 geese in four days.

_____ b. Workers tried to catch the geese with nets.

_____ c. Byrd heard that someone was herding geese with border collies.

4. Making Correct Inferences

Two of the statements below are correct *inferences,* or reasonable guesses. They are based on information in the passage. The other statement is an incorrect, or faulty, inference. Label the statements C for *correct* inference and F for *faulty* inference.

_____ a. Using border collies was a clever solution to a problem.

_____ b. The weather on Buldir is terrible for both people and animals.

_____ c. Aleutian Canada geese now live on other islands besides Buldir.

5. Understanding Main Ideas

One of the statements below expresses the main idea of the passage. One statement is too general, or too broad. The other explains only part of the passage; it is too narrow. Label the statements M for *main idea,* B for *too broad,* and N for *too narrow.*

_____ a. In just four days, the border collies rounded up 143 geese.

_____ b. Aleutian Canada geese are just one of many endangered species of birds.

_____ c. Vernon Byrd solved the problem of rounding up endangered geese by using border collies to herd them.

Correct Answers, Part A _____

Correct Answers, Part B _____

Total Correct Answers _____

Birds of the Air

Almost all the animals that fly belong to two groups, one without and the other with backbones. In the days of the dinosaurs, the birds had backboned rivals in the air. There were many flying reptiles. But times have changed. Birds now outnumber several hundred to one the other vertebrates (those with backbones) that can fly.

Just as there are a few flying vertebrates that are not birds, there are a few birds that cannot fly. Since far back in the time when birds were new on the Earth, there have been some flightless birds. Among the flightless birds of today are the ostriches and kiwis. Most birds, however, can fly at least for a short way. Many are remarkable flyers—they fly both fast and for long distances.

Scientists have timed some birds to find out exactly how fast they can fly. The robin's speed is about 30 miles (48 kilometers) an hour. The chimney swift can fly more than twice as fast.

Wings are needed for real flight. A flying fish can soar through the air for a little way. A flying squirrel can glide from one branch to another. But only creatures with true wings can really fly.

A typical bird's wings are powered by strong wing muscles. On the breastbone, there is a projection called a keel to which the wing muscles are fastened. As it flies, a bird beats its wings against the air and pushes itself forward.

A bird's light weight is a help in flying. A chimney swift weighs less than a mouse or toad of the same size. One reason a bird is so light is that many of its bones are hollow. They are filled with air. Connected with its lungs, a bird also has tiny air sacs throughout its body. These tiny air sacs act like little hot-air balloons.

Many birds use their power of flying to spend their winters in one part of the world and their summers in another. In the northern part of the United States, the appearance of robins is one of the first signs of spring. The robin goes south in the fall and returns in early spring. The chimney swift is a traveler, too. It leaves earlier than the robin in the fall, comes back later in the spring, and travels farther.

Not all birds travel. Some live in one region all their lives.

Reading Time _____

Recalling Facts

1. Birds are
   - ❏ a. vertebrates.
   - ❏ b. animals without backbones.
   - ❏ c. flying reptiles.

2. To really fly, creatures need
   - ❏ a. feathers.
   - ❏ b. real wings.
   - ❏ c. long tails.

3. Many of a bird's bones are
   - ❏ a. filled with water.
   - ❏ b. hollow.
   - ❏ c. like tiny hot-air balloons.

4. A bird's wing muscles are fastened to
   - ❏ a. a bone on its back.
   - ❏ b. each side.
   - ❏ c. a keel on its breastbone.

5. A bird that flies twice as fast as a robin is the
   - ❏ a. kiwi.
   - ❏ b. canary.
   - ❏ c. chimney swift.

Understanding Ideas

6. You can conclude from the article that vertebrates that fly
   - ❏ a. include birds and other animals.
   - ❏ b. are all birds.
   - ❏ c. are mostly animals other than birds.

7. It is likely that the smaller a bird is,
   - ❏ a. the faster it can fly.
   - ❏ b. the more hollow bones it has.
   - ❏ c. the lighter it is.

8. Compared to an animal of the same size, a bird probably weighs
   - ❏ a. about the same.
   - ❏ b. more.
   - ❏ c. less.

9. It is likely that robins fly south in order to
   - ❏ a. get exercise.
   - ❏ b. avoid cold weather.
   - ❏ c. mate.

10. You can conclude that the speed at which different birds fly
    - ❏ a. is about the same.
    - ❏ b. varies from bird to bird.
    - ❏ c. depends mostly on the weather.

11   B   Teaching Birds to Fly

In 1993, William Lishman piloted an ultralight airplane from Ontario, Canada, to Virginia. Behind the plane flew a small flock of young Canada geese. They had been trained to follow the plane as if it were their mother. The geese arrived safely in Virginia. The next spring, without help, they flew back to their Canadian hatching place. The experiment was a success.

Now other wildlife biologists are trying to do the same with sandhill cranes. They hope to lead the birds on a route with safe resting places to a secure winter home. They want the birds to learn the new route. Then they will be able to migrate safely on their own.

The final goal is to teach rare and endangered whooping cranes to migrate along a safe route between Canada and Texas. Fifty years ago, whoopers were nearly extinct. Only twenty birds were alive. Captive breeding programs have increased their numbers to 320. However, most of these birds live in sanctuaries. They do not migrate. A few wild whoopers still make the yearly trip. But the route they learned as young birds is no longer safe. Biologists hope that their experiments with Canada geese and sandhill cranes will help them teach young whoopers to migrate safely.

1. **Recognizing Words in Context**

   Find the word *follow* in the passage. One definition below is a *synonym* for that word; it means the same or almost the same thing. One definition is an *antonym;* it has the opposite or nearly opposite meaning. The other has a completely different meaning. Label the definitions S for *synonym,* A for *antonym,* and D for *different.*

   _____ a. lead

   _____ b. trail

   _____ c. support

2. **Distinguishing Fact from Opinion**

   Two of the statements below present *facts,* which can be proved correct. The other statement is an *opinion,* which expresses someone's thoughts or beliefs. Label the statements F for *fact* and O for *opinion.*

   _____ a. Saving endangered birds is an important task.

   _____ b. Captive breeding has increased whooping crane numbers to 320.

   _____ c. William Lishman piloted an ultralight airplane from Ontario, Canada, to Virginia.

55

3. Keeping Events in Order

Label the statements below 1, 2, and 3 to show the order in which the events happened.

_____ a. The geese migrated back to Canada without help the following year.

_____ b. The geese followed Lishman's plane to Virginia.

_____ c. Lishman trained Canada geese to follow his plane.

4. Making Correct Inferences

Two of the statements below are correct *inferences,* or reasonable guesses. They are based on information in the passage. The other statement is an incorrect, or faulty, inference. Label the statements C for *correct* inference and F for *faulty* inference.

_____ a. Little can be done to save endangered species of birds.

_____ b. Young birds can be trained to follow an airplane.

_____ c. Migrating birds suffer from a lack of safe places to stop and rest.

5. Understanding Main Ideas

One of the statements below expresses the main idea of the passage. One statement is too general, or too broad. The other explains only part of the passage; it is too narrow. Label the statements M for *main idea,* B for *too broad,* and N for *too narrow.*

_____ a. Wildlife biologists are working on ways to teach migrating birds safe routes of travel by training them to follow ultralight aircraft.

_____ b. A key part of the long-range recovery plan for whooping cranes is to establish new, safe migratory routes.

_____ c. The migratory route wild whooping cranes follow from Canada to Texas is no longer safe.

Correct Answers, Part A _____

Correct Answers, Part B _____

Total Correct Answers _____

Rabbits and Hares

Among the best-known wild animals are the cottontails and jackrabbits. They are abundant in the brushy woods and gardens of eastern North America, on the western plains and deserts, on mountains, and even in the Arctic snows.

Many of the animals called rabbits are actually hares. The hare is larger and heavier and has longer ears. With its longer hind legs and larger hind feet, it can outjump any rabbit and does not tire as quickly. Many hares turn white in the winter. Rabbits keep the same color coat year-round.

Hares and rabbits bear their young in very different ways. The female hare (called a doe) has two or three litters of young a year, with from four to six babies in each litter. She does not make a nest. The young are born in a flattened area called a form, in the grass beneath a low branch, or under a brush heap. Young jackrabbits, which are hares, may lie directly on the desert ground in the shade of a cactus or other plant. Young hares are born with their eyes open and with dense fur on their bodies. They can care for themselves within a few days.

A mother rabbit provides a nest by scraping out a hollow in the grass or moving into an old woodchuck hole. The young are born blind, naked, and helpless. The mother feeds the babies with her milk. When she goes for her own food, she hides the nest with leaves or grass. The baby rabbits open their eyes in about a week. In ten or 12 days, they leave the nest. By the time they are 3 weeks old, they can care for themselves. Rabbits have many litters from early spring to late fall. There are from four to six young in each litter. In the southern states, rabbits bear young throughout the year. Male rabbits and hares (called bucks) pay no attention to the young.

Rabbits and hares are gnawing animals like rats, mice, and squirrels. They have the same type of strong, chisel-like front teeth.

Rabbits and hares feed at night and remain in the nest or form during the day. They are fond of all green growing things and have thus earned the reputation of doing great damage to gardens and field crops. In the winter, they feed on the bark of trees and shrubs, on buds, and on berries.

Reading Time _____

Recalling Facts

1. Compared to rabbits, hares are
   - ❑ a. smaller and less quick.
   - ❑ b. larger and heavier.
   - ❑ c. short-eared.

2. The female hare is called a
   - ❑ a. jackrabbit.
   - ❑ b. doe.
   - ❑ c. nurse.

3. Young hares become independent
   - ❑ a. within a few days.
   - ❑ b. within a year.
   - ❑ c. after a year.

4. In a year, rabbits have
   - ❑ a. one litter.
   - ❑ b. two litters.
   - ❑ c. many litters.

5. Male rabbits are known for
   - ❑ a. protecting their young.
   - ❑ b. ignoring their young.
   - ❑ c. eating their young.

Understanding Ideas

6. Compared to young rabbits, young hares
   - ❑ a. are independent sooner.
   - ❑ b. are dependent longer.
   - ❑ c. leave the nest later.

7. It is likely that the dense fur on the bodies of young hares
   - ❑ a. constantly changes color.
   - ❑ b. falls out as they age.
   - ❑ c. helps to protect them.

8. You can conclude from the article that a mother rabbit
   - ❑ a. must be very protective of her young.
   - ❑ b. pays little attention to her young.
   - ❑ c. pushes her young out of the nest.

9. It is likely that rabbits and hares feed at night because
   - ❑ a. it is cooler.
   - ❑ b. it is easier to conceal themselves from enemies.
   - ❑ c. food is more plentiful then.

10. You can conclude that rabbits and hares
    - ❑ a. are becoming scarce.
    - ❑ b. live only in warmer climates.
    - ❑ c. are very adaptable creatures.

The Hare with Many Friends

An Aesop Fable

There was once a hare who had many friends. She thought she was the most popular animal in the entire world!

One day the hare heard hounds baying in the distance. Usually, she hurried away at the first sound of a baying dog, but this time she asked herself, "Why should I have to run for my life every time I hear a dog?" She decided her friends could help. She would ask one of them to carry her to safety.

The hare asked the horse, "Please, dear friend, will you carry me away from the hounds?"

The horse answered, "I wish I could assist you, but I have work to do for my owner." Next the hare asked the cow for help. The cow answered, "I wish I could help you, but it's almost milking time."

The goat was busy, too. So were the sheep and the pig. Every animal the rabbit asked for help seemed to be occupied. Even the calf had no time for her. Each one said, "I wish I could help you." But all of them had some excuse that prevented them from helping her. By this time, the hounds were getting closer. The hare didn't have any time to spare. She was forced to run for her life. She quickly took off and, luckily, escaped just in time.

The moral of this fable is those who have many friends have no friends.

1. **Recognizing Words in Context**

   Find the word *hounds* in the passage. One definition below is a *synonym* for that word; it means the same or almost the same thing. One definition is an *antonym;* it has the opposite or nearly opposite meaning. The other has a completely different meaning. Label the definitions S for *synonym,* A for *antonym,* and D for *different.*

   _____ a. chases

   _____ b. dogs

   _____ c. cats

2. **Distinguishing Fact from Opinion**

   Two of the statements below present *facts,* which can be proved correct. The other statement is an *opinion,* which expresses someone's thoughts or beliefs. Label the statements F for *fact* and O for *opinion.*

   _____ a. The hare heard hounds baying in the distance.

   _____ b. The hare was the most popular animal in the world.

   _____ c. All of the hare's friends were too busy to help her.

3. Keeping Events in Order

Label the statements below 1, 2, and 3 to show the order in which the events happened.

_____ a. The cow told the hare that it was milking time.

_____ b. The horse told the hare it had work to do for its owner.

_____ c. The hare decided that she had better run for her life.

4. Making Correct Inferences

Two of the statements below are correct *inferences,* or reasonable guesses. They are based on information in the passage. The other statement is an incorrect, or faulty, inference. Label the statements C for *correct* inference and F for *faulty* inference.

_____ a. The hounds were also friends of the hare.

_____ b. The other animals were not true friends of the hare.

_____ c. If the hare had not run off, the hounds might have killed her.

5. Understanding Main Ideas

One of the statements below expresses the main idea of the passage. One statement is too general, or too broad. The other explains only part of the passage; it is too narrow. Label the statements M for *main idea,* B for *too broad,* and N for *too narrow.*

_____ a. Dogs are one of the many enemies of hares and rabbits.

_____ b. The hare decided that rather than run away from the hounds, she would ask her friends to help her escape from them.

_____ c. A hare who thinks she has many friends discovers in a time of crisis that she has no friends.

Correct Answers, Part A _____

Correct Answers, Part B _____

Total Correct Answers _____

Life of a Logger

Early loggers led an unsettled life, wandering from one job to another. Many stayed at a logging camp for only a few days or weeks. Their work was hard and long. They were free only on Sundays and evenings. Loggers worked 11 hours a day until their workday was reduced to ten hours in 1910. After 1920, loggers worked eight hours a day, five days a week. Usually they worked even in rain, snow, and freezing cold. If bad weather did stop work, they were not paid for lost time.

A typical logging camp contained a bunkhouse, a cookhouse, a dining room, and an office. There were stables and a blacksmith's shop and perhaps a store, a meat house, and storage sheds. The number of buildings depended on the number of workers and on the kind of equipment to be stored and maintained.

The bunkhouses were rude buildings that had tiers of bunks nailed to the walls. There was just room enough between a bunk and the one above it for a worker to crawl into bed and roll over. Often double bunks were used. One worker would be assigned to each side. Blankets and sometimes a straw mattress were furnished. Otherwise the workers made do with spruce boughs. Bedbugs were a common complaint. A stove in the middle of the room provided heat. After working in the rain or snow or doing their laundry, the loggers hung their clothes around the stove to dry. Smoke from the stove mixed with steam from the wet clothes.

The day began at 5:00 A.M. when the bull cook (the camp odd-jobs worker) woke the loggers. At 5:30, the gong sounded for the huge breakfast that prepared them for the day's work. The cook was one of the most important and best-paid workers in the camp. The meals made had to satisfy the ravenous appetites of the hardworking loggers. If they did not like their food, they might refuse to work.

At 9:00 P.M., the lights were turned out. The workers immediately went to bed and were quiet. They needed plenty of rest just as they needed plenty of food.

Loggers whose homes were near the camp could leave it on Saturday evening and return on Sunday. The others could not leave until payday. Most evenings were spent playing cards or spinning yarns (telling made-up stories). Many legends grew out of these loggers' tales.

Reading Time _____

Recalling Facts

1. An early logger's workday lasted
   - ❏ a. 9 hours.
   - ❏ b. 11 hours.
   - ❏ c. 15 hours.

2. Loggers slept in
   - ❏ a. stables.
   - ❏ b. tents.
   - ❏ c. bunkhouses.

3. A logger's workday began at
   - ❏ a. 3:00 A.M.
   - ❏ b. 5:00 A.M.
   - ❏ c. 9:00 A.M.

4. The job of a bull cook in a logging camp was to
   - ❏ a. perform odd jobs.
   - ❏ b. slaughter bulls for cooking.
   - ❏ c. cook breakfast.

5. The loggers' workday was reduced to 8 hours in
   - ❏ a. the 1800s.
   - ❏ b. 1910.
   - ❏ c. the 1920s.

Understanding Ideas

6. It is likely that early loggers
   - ❏ a. were envied for their jobs.
   - ❏ b. were well paid.
   - ❏ c. received low wages.

7. You can conclude from the article that conditions in logging camps today
   - ❏ a. have changed little from the early days.
   - ❏ b. have improved over those of the early days.
   - ❏ c. are worse than in the early days.

8. You can conclude that a typical logging camp included
   - ❏ a. horses.
   - ❏ b. cars.
   - ❏ c. bicycles.

9. It is likely that loggers' yarns came from
   - ❏ a. books they had read.
   - ❏ b. their imaginations.
   - ❏ c. historical events.

10. Logging camps were most likely located
    - ❏ a. in forested areas.
    - ❏ b. by the ocean.
    - ❏ c. in areas with warm climates.

According to legend, the greatest logger of all was Paul Bunyan. Soon after he dug the St. Lawrence River, Paul got a letter from the king of Sweden asking him to cut down all the trees in North Dakota so that Swedes could settle there. The king wanted the job done in one month, in time for planting.

Paul built his biggest camp ever. The bunks had eighteen levels. The loggers on the top had to get up an hour earlier than those lower down in order to reach bottom in time for breakfast.

The project seemed beset by bad luck. A fog rolled in so thick that even the fish got confused. They swam up into it! At night, the loggers had to wrap themselves in mosquito nets to keep fish out of their ears. When the fog lifted, there were fish all over the forest.

The job was done on time, but one problem remained—all the tree stumps. Paul had Babe, his huge blue ox, step on each stump. Babe's great weight drove the stumps six feet into the ground. The farmers could plant, and the king was happy. Even better, without the trees, Babe had room to lie down.

1. **Recognizing Words in Context**

    Find the word *settle* in the passage. One definition below is a *synonym* for that word; it means the same or almost the same thing. One definition is an *antonym;* it has the opposite or nearly opposite meaning. The other has a completely different meaning. Label the definitions S for *synonym*, A for *antonym,* and D for *different*.

    _____ a. live

    _____ b. sink

    _____ c. leave

2. **Distinguishing Fact from Opinion**

    Two of the statements below present *facts*, which can be proved correct. The other statement is an *opinion,* which expresses someone's thoughts or beliefs. Label the statements F for *fact* and O for *opinion.*

    _____ a. Paul Bunyan's ox was named Babe.

    _____ b. A legend says that Paul Bunyan cut down all the trees in North Dakota.

    _____ c. Paul Bunyan was the greatest logger of all.

3. Keeping Events in Order

Label the statements below 1, 2, and 3 to show the order in which the events happened.

_____ a. The loggers had to wrap themselves in mosquito nets to keep the fish out of their ears.

_____ b. When the fog lifted, fish were all over the forest.

_____ c. Fish were confused by the heavy fog and swam up into it.

4. Making Correct Inferences

Two of the statements below are correct *inferences,* or reasonable guesses. They are based on information in the passage. The other statement is an incorrect, or faulty, inference. Label the statements C for *correct* inference and F for *faulty* inference.

_____ a. This story is a tall tale.

_____ b. This story is a way of explaining things about nature and geography.

_____ c. Paul Bunyan was a real person.

5. Understanding Main Ideas

One of the statements below expresses the main idea of the passage. One statement is too general, or too broad. The other explains only part of the passage; it is too narrow. Label the statements M for *main idea,* B for *too broad,* and N for *too narrow.*

_____ a. Paul Bunyan and his logging crew cleared away all the trees in North Dakota so that Swedish farmers could settle there.

_____ b. Paul Bunyan responded to a request from the king of Sweden by building the largest logging camp ever.

_____ c. Many different tales have been told about Paul Bunyan.

Correct Answers, Part A _____

Correct Answers, Part B _____

Total Correct Answers _____

Almost everyone has heard about glaciers, but most Americans have never seen one. Most would say that they are rare. Some people think glaciers are found only in the far north. Are they really so rare? Are they a possible source of water? Think about these facts.

About three-fourths of all the fresh water in the world is stored as glacier ice. This is about the same as 60 years of rainfall all over the globe. In North America, there is more water stored as snow and ice in glaciers than in all its lakes, ponds, rivers, and reservoirs.

What is a glacier? Any large mass of snow and ice on land, which lasts for many years, may be called a glacier. Glaciers form when more snow falls than melts over the years. The snow packs down and becomes thick. As it is pressed down, it changes into solid ice. Eventually, this mass of snow and ice gets very heavy. When this happens, it starts to move. When a glacier forms on a slope, it moves downhill. When it is on a flat area, it moves out in all directions.

Glaciers take several forms. Some are found in shells carved out of mountains by the ice itself. Others are found in ridges where much snow is carried by wind drift. Several large valley glaciers join at the foot of a mountain range in Alaska. Large glaciers are also found in Greenland and Antarctica. They are similar to the ice sheets that covered much of North America during the Ice Age.

About three percent of Alaska is covered by glaciers. Most of them are in mountains not far from the big cities. The runoff of glacial waters affects life in Alaska. Most of the large rivers start with the glaciers. The glaciers are an important water source to Alaska. The water is stored in the glaciers during the winter when the need for water is not so great. In the heat of the summer when the need is greatest, the water melts. It becomes available for use.

Where are the best glaciers? To see them in all their varied shapes and sizes, one should travel to Alaska. Air routes fly over or very near some of the largest glaciers in North America. In the United States south of Alaska, the best places to see glaciers is in Mount Rainier National Park.

Reading Time _____

Recalling Facts

1. Glacial ice makes up
   - ❏ a. most of the fresh water in the world.
   - ❏ b. about half of the fresh water in the world.
   - ❏ c. most of the world's salt water.

2. A glacier can be defined as a
   - ❏ a. frozen body of water.
   - ❏ b. small mass of snow and ice in the sea.
   - ❏ c. large, long-lasting mass of snow and ice on land.

3. The percentage of Alaska that is covered by glaciers is about
   - ❏ a. three percent.
   - ❏ b. fifteen percent.
   - ❏ c. fifty percent.

4. Most of Alaska's glaciers are found in
   - ❏ a. big cities.
   - ❏ b. mountains near big cities.
   - ❏ c. remote areas.

5. The best place to see glaciers south of Alaska is
   - ❏ a. Greenland
   - ❏ b. Antarctica.
   - ❏ c. Mount Rainier National Park.

Understanding Ideas

6. You can conclude from the article that Alaska has
   - ❏ a. the world's largest glaciers.
   - ❏ b. the most varied glaciers.
   - ❏ c. more glaciers than any other location.

7. You can conclude that glaciers are located
   - ❏ a. in few parts of the United States.
   - ❏ b. nowhere in the United States.
   - ❏ c. in most parts of the United States.

8. The article suggests that glaciers should be regarded as
   - ❏ a. a valuable source of water.
   - ❏ b. a danger to big cities.
   - ❏ c. a rare tourist attraction.

9. The average American's idea of glaciers is probably
   - ❏ a. accurate.
   - ❏ b. different from most people's.
   - ❏ c. not based on fact.

10. You can conclude that glaciers are found mainly in areas
    - ❏ a. with year-round freezing temperatures.
    - ❏ b. with large mountain ranges.
    - ❏ c. where the temperature is cold for a good part of the year.

A Glacier Walk

The first thing our guide did was check to see that our crampons were secure. These were spiked metal plates, attached to our boots with straps, that could grip ice. "Stay together," he said. Then he led us out onto the glacier.

We left summer behind and crunched across a surface that looked like tiny ice cubes.

The ice was full of dirt and pebbles. In some places it was streaked with blue that the guide said was minerals. He led us around bumps and hollows that might be unsafe. Everything was strange and still, with no signs of animals or plants. The guide took us to the edge of a deep crack and let us look down. We couldn't see the bottom. Sometimes, he told us, cracks like this open up suddenly without warning. Then he took us to a place where melted snow ran under the glacier's surface. We looked into a hole and saw a rushing river below.

At the end of the hike, the guide dug steps in the glacier's icy side so we could climb down and walk back to the hotel. At first, the ground was stony and dead looking. Then we saw the first tiny mosses and then low plants. Finally, we were back in summer again.

1. **Recognizing Words in Context**

   Find the word *stony* in the passage. One definition below is a *synonym* for that word; it means the same or almost the same thing. One definition is an *antonym;* it has the opposite or nearly opposite meaning. The other has a completely different meaning. Label the definitions S for *synonym*, A for *antonym*, and D for *different*.

   _____ a. unfeeling

   _____ b. soft

   _____ c. rocky

2. **Distinguishing Fact from Opinion**

   Two of the statements below present *facts*, which can be proved correct. The other statement is an *opinion*, which expresses someone's thoughts or beliefs. Label the statements F for *fact* and O for *opinion*.

   _____ a. Everything was strange and still.

   _____ b. The ice was full of dirt and pebbles.

   _____ c. Crampons are spiked metal plates that can grip ice.

3. **Keeping Events in Order**

Label the statements below 1, 2, and 3 to show the order in which the events happened.

_____ a. The guide told everyone to stay together.

_____ b. The guide dug steps in the ice.

_____ c. The hikers looked down a deep crack.

4. **Making Correct Inferences**

Two of the statements below are correct *inferences,* or reasonable guesses. They are based on information in the passage. The other statement is an incorrect, or faulty, inference. Label the statements C for *correct* inference and F for *faulty* inference.

_____ a. With a guide, there is no danger in a glacier walk.

_____ b. Glaciers can be dangerous places.

_____ c. Nothing can live on a glacier.

5. **Understanding Main Ideas**

One of the statements below expresses the main idea of the passage. One statement is too general, or too broad. The other explains only part of the passage; it is too narrow. Label the statements M for *main idea*, B for *too broad,* and N for *too narrow.*

_____ a. The surface of the glacier looked like tiny ice cubes, full of dirt and pebbles.

_____ b. On a glacier walk, hikers learn from a guide about the special features of a glacier.

_____ c. Ten percent of the Earth's land surface is covered by glaciers. ·

Correct Answers, Part A _____

Correct Answers, Part B _____

Total Correct Answers _____

Swim Safely

Swimming is enjoyed by people of all ages, from the very young to the very old. All over the world people swim for fun. There are many places where people can enjoy swimming. People swim in lakes, oceans, and rivers. Some swim in pools. Many schools, motels, apartment buildings, and clubs have indoor or outdoor pools. Some families have pools in their yards.

Swimming is one of the best forms of exercise. It can improve heart action. It also helps blood circulate. Swimming will develop strong muscles. It will even strengthen the lungs. People who are disabled and can't enjoy other sports can keep their bodies in better condition by swimming.

It is a good idea for parents to make sure that their children learn to swim at an early age. This will be an activity that the children can enjoy for the rest of their lives.

There are basic rules for water safety that can help save your life. These rules can also help you save the life of a friend.

First of all, know how to swim. Many schools give lessons to children as part of their athletic program. Adults can learn to swim at public pools or recreation centers.

Another rule to remember is never swim alone. Always swim with a friend and know where that person is in the water at all times. It is best to swim only in places where there is a lifeguard. If you swim in the ocean or a river, it is good to know about tides and currents.

Whether you are a beginner or an experienced swimmer, it is good to know survival bobbing. This can help you if there is an accident. Survival bobbing lets you float for a long time on your stomach. This bobbing uses very little energy. You fill your lungs with air. At the same time, you relax your body. Your arms and legs hang down limply, and your chin flops down to your chest. The air in your lungs will hold your head above the water. When you need a breath, you breathe out through your nose. Then you lift your face out of the water and breathe in through your mouth. You then return to the restful floating position.

Never take dangerous chances when swimming. Most drownings could be avoided if everyone knew how to swim and followed the basic rules for water safety.

Reading Time _____

Recalling Facts

1. Swimming can help improve
   - ❏ a. heart action.
   - ❏ b. eyesight.
   - ❏ c. hearing.

2. An important rule in swimming is
   - ❏ a. swim in deep water.
   - ❏ b. never swim alone.
   - ❏ c. always float.

3. Survival bobbing means
   - ❏ a. floating on your back.
   - ❏ b. pushing up and down with your legs.
   - ❏ c. floating on your stomach.

4. It is best to swim in
   - ❏ a. swimming pools.
   - ❏ b. places where there is a lifeguard.
   - ❏ c. lakes.

5. Swimming can help develop
   - ❏ a. strong muscles.
   - ❏ b. memory.
   - ❏ c. creative ability.

Understanding Ideas

6. The more air that is in your lungs, the more
   - ❏ a. you will sink.
   - ❏ b. you will float.
   - ❏ c. your body will weigh.

7. Survival bobbing should be learned
   - ❏ a. by anyone who swims.
   - ❏ b. by beginner swimmers only.
   - ❏ c. only as a last resort.

8. You can conclude from the article that the best way to avoid drowning is to
   - ❏ a. swim in pools.
   - ❏ b. swim in shallow water.
   - ❏ c. follow the basic rules for water safety.

9. The article suggests that swimming is
   - ❏ a. beneficial for most people.
   - ❏ b. a dangerous sport.
   - ❏ c. life-threatening.

10. You can conclude that teaching children to swim at an early age
    - ❏ a. helps save lives.
    - ❏ b. teaches good moral values.
    - ❏ c. is bad for their health.

When you are 74 years old, starting anything new is a big thing. Who would ever take up synchronized swimming at that age? Fred Wing did. Fred's wife, Louise, had been an expert synchro swimmer as a young woman. At 68, she was still interested in the sport. She wanted Fred to try it.

Synchronized swimming is water ballet. The swimmers perform acrobatic movements underwater and on the surface to music. It is beautiful to watch. It also takes a lot of practice. Fred could swim, but he had never done synchro swimming. During warm weather, he and Louise practiced in a lake. The rest of the year, they swam in a community center pool. There were always other swimmers in the pool. Lap swimmers had the right of way, so Fred and Louise often had to move. Finally, the center slotted one hour a week in the pool just for synchro swimming.

At first, organizers of synchro swimming competitions said the Wings were too old to compete. There was no master's division as there is in other sports. Louise campaigned to change this. A master's division was finally established. Less than two years after Fred began, the Wings became the U.S. synchro swimming master's champions.

1. **Recognizing Words in Context**

   Find the word *division* in the passage. One definition below is a *synonym* for that word; it means the same or almost the same thing. One definition is an *antonym;* it has the opposite or nearly opposite meaning. The other has a completely different meaning. Label the definitions S for *synonym,* A for *antonym,* and D for *different.*

   _____ a. whole

   _____ b. separation

   _____ c. section

2. **Distinguishing Fact from Opinion**

   Two of the statements below present *facts,* which can be proved correct. The other statement is an *opinion,* which expresses someone's thoughts or beliefs. Label the statements F for *fact* and O for *opinion.*

   _____ a. Fred Wing took up synchronized swimming at the age of 74.

   _____ b. The Wings were too old to compete.

   _____ c. Louise had been a synchro swimmer as a young woman.

3. Keeping Events in Order

Label the statements below 1, 2, and 3 to show the order in which the events happened.

_____ a. Synchro swimming competitions had no division for older swimmers.

_____ b. Fred and Louise became master's synchro swimming champions.

_____ c. A master's division in synchro swimming was established.

4. Making Correct Inferences

Two of the statements below are correct *inferences*, or reasonable guesses. They are based on information in the passage. The other statement is an incorrect, or faulty, inference. Label the statements C for *correct* inference and F for *faulty* inference.

_____ a. Age alone does not prevent a person from taking up a new activity.

_____ b. There was no master's division in synchro swimming because competition organizers did not want older swimmers to be injured.

_____ c. Fred and Louise are excellent synchro swimmers.

5. Understanding Main Ideas

One of the statements below expresses the main idea of the passage. One statement is too general, or too broad. The other explains only part of the passage; it is too narrow. Label the statements M for *main idea,* B for *too broad,* and N for *too narrow.*

_____ a. Fred Wing took up synchronized swimming at the age of 74, and he and his wife became master's champions.

_____ b. Synchronized swimming is water ballet.

_____ c. Louise Wing wanted her husband, Fred, to try synchro swimming.

Correct Answers, Part A _____

Correct Answers, Part B _____

Total Correct Answers _____

Pesticides are chemicals that kill. They can slow or stop the growth of pests. Pests can be insects, fish, rats, mice, fungi, weeds, and other harmful animals or plants. Some pests spoil food. Some ruin clothes, household goods, and buildings. Pests can spread disease. They can injure and kill people. Pests can also harm helpful animals and plants.

Helpful animals and plants are those that people like and use. Or they are ones that are vital to a healthy world. Some might be living things that are used as food. These include vegetables, grains, fruits, chickens, and cattle. They could be the houseplants that help make a home pleasant. Some are the cats and dogs and other animals that people keep as pets. These are just some of the animals and plants that people enjoy. There are also some forms of life that help keep a smooth and even balance in nature. Pests can destroy these useful plants and animals. So, to help protect them, people use pesticides.

Pesticides can help control pests. But they can cause harm, too. People may not follow the directions carefully when using them. When this happens, people can harm the animals and plants that they want to protect. Pesticides are poisons. The deadly effects of these poisons can last a long time. The remains of some pesticides last for many years. They harm and kill long after they were first used.

Pesticides are useful when used correctly. They help protect people and useful plants and animals. They destroy unwanted plants and animals. But if not used in the right way, pesticides can cause a great deal of harm. Someone who uses pesticides can never be too careful.

Guard yourself and others from pesticides. It is especially important to keep pesticides out of the reach of children. It is not safe for children to use them. In some states, it is against the law. Pest control is a job for adults.

Children should be able to know a pesticide by the label on the package. Children should be taught not to use empty pesticide jars or cans. Spilled pesticide on the outside of a jar can be unsafe. It can poison someone. Keep poisons out of the reach of small children.

Sometimes people are poisoned by a pesticide. If this happens, be sure to follow the directions on the label. Also get medical help.

Reading Time _____

Recalling Facts

1. Pesticides
   - ❏ a. spread disease.
   - ❏ b. provide plants with vitamins.
   - ❏ c. slow or stop the growth of pests.

2. People use pesticides to
   - ❏ a. protect helpful plants and animals.
   - ❏ b. harm helpful plants and animals.
   - ❏ c. feed plants and animals.

3. Pests are defined as
   - ❏ a. harmful animals or plants.
   - ❏ b. chemicals that can kill.
   - ❏ c. useful animals or plants.

4. In some states, it is against the law to
   - ❏ a. use pesticides.
   - ❏ b. let children use pesticides.
   - ❏ c. spill pesticides.

5. Pesticide users should be careful to
   - ❏ a. use them only at night.
   - ❏ b. follow the directions.
   - ❏ c. wear light clothing.

Understanding Ideas

6. You can conclude from the article that the effects of pesticides
   - ❏ a. are usually short-lived.
   - ❏ b. cannot always be controlled.
   - ❏ c. are not harmful to people.

7. You can conclude that pesticides must
   - ❏ a. be carefully used.
   - ❏ b. be banned.
   - ❏ c. not be limited.

8. The main idea of the article is that pesticides are
   - ❏ a. mostly useful.
   - ❏ b. mostly harmful.
   - ❏ c. both useful and harmful.

9. You can conclude that people consider plants and animals
   - ❏ a. helpful.
   - ❏ b. harmful.
   - ❏ c. helpful or harmful.

10. The purpose of this article is to
    - ❏ a. entertain.
    - ❏ b. inform.
    - ❏ c. persuade.

People thought DDT was a miracle. First used in 1939, DDT killed insects that damaged crops. The new pesticide was effective against many destructive insects. It worked against mosquitoes, fleas, moths, and beetles. Before long, DDT became a regular weapon in farmers' war on insects. Farmers knew that it killed pests. They did not know about other effects of DDT. Over time, it built up in the soil. Soil polluted with DDT was washed into streams by the rain. The pesticide also built up in the bodies of animals.

No one noticed when fish began to die. No one noticed there were fewer and fewer birds each spring. Then in 1962, biologist and science writer Rachel Carson wrote *Silent Spring*. In her book, Carson linked the dying off of birds to the "miracle" pesticide DDT. The powerful chemical industry said that Carson was wrong. Studies proved, however, that DDT weakened the eggshells of birds. Birds were dying off in such numbers that "silent spring" was becoming a reality.

In 1971, the United States finally banned DDT. As a result, many bird populations began recovering. Carson's warning helped save the birds before it was too late. However, Carson did not live to see the birds recover. She died in 1964, less than two years after *Silent Spring* was published.

1. **Recognizing Words in Context**

    Find the word *linked* in the passage. One definition below is a *synonym* for that word; it means the same or almost the same thing. One definition is an *antonym;* it has the opposite or nearly opposite meaning. The other has a completely different meaning. Label the definitions S for *synonym,* A for *antonym,* and D for *different.*

    _____ a. bound

    _____ b. separated

    _____ c. connected

2. **Distinguishing Fact from Opinion**

    Two of the statements below present *facts,* which can be proved correct. The other statement is an *opinion,* which expresses someone's thoughts or beliefs. Label the statements F for *fact* and O for *opinion.*

    _____ a. DDT was effective against many insect pests.

    _____ b. DDT was a miracle pesticide.

    _____ c. DDT weakened the eggshells of birds.

3. Keeping Events in Order

Label the statements below 1, 2, and 3 to show the order in which the events happened.

_____ a. Rachel Carson wrote the book *Silent Spring*.

_____ b. Birds and fish began dying off.

_____ c. Farmers began using DDT against insect pests.

4. Making Correct Inferences

Two of the statements below are correct *inferences*, or reasonable guesses. They are based on information in the passage. The other statement is an incorrect, or faulty, inference. Label the statements C for *correct* inference and F for *faulty* inference.

_____ a. DDT caused only harmful effects, not good effects.

_____ b. DDT washed into water from soil was killing off fish.

_____ c. Weakened eggshells meant that baby birds did not develop properly.

5. Understanding Main Ideas

One of the statements below expresses the main idea of the passage. One statement is too general, or too broad. The other explains only part of the passage; it is too narrow. Label the statements M for *main idea*, B for *too broad*, and N for *too narrow*.

_____ a. In *Silent Spring*, biologist Rachel Carson showed that the pesticide DDT was related to a decline in bird populations.

_____ b. Pesticides are chemicals that can slow or stop the growth of pests.

_____ c. DDT killed insect pests that damaged crops.

Correct Answers, Part A _____

Correct Answers, Part B _____

Total Correct Answers _____

Early people hunted with the bow more than 8,000 years ago. Bows and arrows are one of humans' oldest weapons. They were an important discovery for people. It gave them a deadly weapon with which they could kill their enemies. They could also kill prey from a distance.

The ordinary bow, or short bow, was used by nearly all early people. This bow had limited power and a short range. However, early hunters overcame these faults by learning to track their prey at close range. In fact, some African pygmies still hunt this way. They get very close to their prey and then shoot it with poisoned arrows. Too, North American Indians rarely tried a shot more than forty yards away.

The longbow was most likely invented when someone found out that a five-foot (1.5-meter) piece of wood made a better bow than a three-foot (0.9-meter) piece. The final length of the longbow was probably six feet, six inches (about 2 meters). Hundreds of thousands of these bows were made and used for 300 years. However, not one is known to have survived until today. A force of about 100 pounds (45 kilograms) was needed to pull the string of the longbow all the way back. Anyone who used this bow had to be strong.

The English longbow arrows were made of oak, ash, or birch. The arrows were usually feathered with wing feathers from the gray goose. The arrowheads were made of steel. They were broad and barbed. The archer carried twenty-four such arrows into battle. Archers could shoot one every five seconds if they had to. This made them a fearful enemy.

For a long time, the bow was just a bent stick and a string. In fact, more changes have taken place in the bow and arrow in the past twenty-five years than in the last seven centuries. Today's bow is forceful. It is as exact as a gun. Plus, little strength is needed to draw the string. Modern bows also have fine sights. An expert can hit a bull's-eye many times in a row from a good distance away. In indoor contests, perfect scores from forty yards are common. Matches have been lost when a winning arrow was stopped by one already in the bull's-eye.

The invention of the bow ranks with the discovery of fire and the wheel. It was a great step forward for humans.

Reading Time _____

Recalling Facts

1. Nearly all early people hunted with
   - ❏ a. slingshots.
   - ❏ b. nets.
   - ❏ c. short bows.

2. The length of the longbow is estimated at about
   - ❏ a. three feet (0.9 meters).
   - ❏ b. six and a half feet (about 2 meters).
   - ❏ c. ten feet (3 meters).

3. The longbow's main disadvantage was
   - ❏ a. the strength required to use it.
   - ❏ b. that it did not survive.
   - ❏ c. that it did not shoot straight.

4. Most of the changes in the bow and arrow were made
   - ❏ a. in the last twenty-five years.
   - ❏ b. one hundred years ago.
   - ❏ c. centuries ago.

5. Indoor bow-and-arrow contests are won by hitting
   - ❏ a. the outer edge of the target.
   - ❏ b. the bull's-eye.
   - ❏ c. objects tossed in the air.

Understanding Ideas

6. Bows probably came about as a result of
   - ❏ a. scientific experimentation.
   - ❏ b. a lack of gunpowder.
   - ❏ c. trial and error.

7. It is likely that American Indians did not try to use a short bow to shoot arrows past forty yards because
   - ❏ a. they were poor shots.
   - ❏ b. the bow was not accurate at greater distances.
   - ❏ c. they were not strong enough.

8. You can conclude from the article that longer bows are generally
   - ❏ a. more accurate than shorter bows.
   - ❏ b. more difficult to use than shorter bows.
   - ❏ c. more expensive than shorter bows.

9. The short bow and longbow most likely get their names from
   - ❏ a. the range of the bow.
   - ❏ b. the height of the person using the weapon.
   - ❏ c. the length of the bow.

10. You can conclude that the invention of the bow is considered
    - ❏ a. an invention of great importance.
    - ❏ b. the greatest invention in history.
    - ❏ c. more important than the invention of the wheel or fire.

Jim Welch, Bowmaker

Jim Welch is a Native-American bowmaker. He played with bows and arrows as a child. When he grew up, he decided to try to build a traditional bow like those used by eastern North American Indians. He learned, however, that the art of bowmaking had mostly been lost.

Welch went to museums to look at bows and tried to figure out how they had been made. He talked to other bowmakers. Although bows look simple, they are not. A bow is carved from one piece of wood that can stretch on one side and bend inward on the other without breaking. When bent, it must snap back to its original shape. Welch kept experimenting. He tried different woods. He broke many bows that he had carved too thin or too thick.

After he had been making bows for ten years, Jim Welch became a full-time bowmaker. He can make about two bows a week. He tests every bow he makes by shooting it a hundred times before he sells it.

Jim Welch does something else. He teaches other Native Americans to make bows in the traditional way. By this means, he returns to other North American Indians knowledge of their culture that was almost lost.

1. **Recognizing Words in Context**

Find the word *lost* in the passage. One definition below is a *synonym* for that word; it means the same or almost the same thing. One definition is an *antonym*; it has the opposite or nearly opposite meaning. The other has a completely different meaning. Label the definitions S for *synonym*, A for *antonym*, and D for *different*.

_____ a. misplaced

_____ b. remembered

_____ c. forgotten

2. **Distinguishing Fact from Opinion**

Two of the statements below present *facts*, which can be proved correct. The other statement is an *opinion*, which expresses someone's thoughts or beliefs. Label the statements F for *fact* and O for *opinion*.

_____ a. Jim Welch tried different woods for the bows he made.

_____ b. Welch tests each bow by shooting it a hundred times.

_____ c. It is tragic when traditional skills are lost.

3. Keeping Events in Order

Label the statements below 1, 2, and 3 to show the order in which the events happened.

_____ a. Welch studied bows in museums.

_____ b. Welch became a full-time bowmaker.

_____ c. Jim Welch decided to make a traditional bow.

4. Making Correct Inferences

Two of the statements below are correct *inferences,* or reasonable guesses. They are based on information in the passage. The other statement is an incorrect, or faulty, inference. Label the statements C for *correct* inference and F for *faulty* inference.

_____ a. The lost art of bowmaking can never be recovered.

_____ b. Welch is an excellent craftsperson.

_____ c. Bows were important to Native-American culture.

5. Understanding Main Ideas

One of the statements below expresses the main idea of the passage. One statement is too general, or too broad. The other explains only part of the passage; it is too narrow. Label the statements M for *main idea,* B for *too broad,* and N for *too narrow.*

_____ a. When he wanted to make a traditional bow, Jim Welch learned that the art of bowmaking had been mostly lost.

_____ b. Jim Welch taught himself to make bows in the traditional Native-American way and became a full-time bowmaker.

_____ c. Bows and arrows are one of people's oldest weapons.

Correct Answers, Part A _____

Correct Answers, Part B _____

Total Correct Answers _____

The Ships of Salem

Farming was hard in New England. Many a New Englander left the plow to seek fortune on the sea. The people of Salem, a small town in Massachusetts, were no exception. At first they were fishers, going far out to sea for codfish. Then they began sailing their little schooners south to the West Indies. There they exchanged codfish and lumber for salt, sugar, or molasses. Often they went to ports on the Mediterranean. Sometimes they made it to the coasts of Africa.

When the Revolutionary War came, the people of Salem went out in larger ships. These ships, called privateers, attacked the ships of Britain. When the war was over, Salem was left with 158 privateers. These vessels were too large for the West Indies trade. Besides, Britain ruled the West Indies. Americans could no longer do business there. And so Salem sent its ships to the East. They sailed to China, India, and the lands of the East Indies.

And Salem sent its children, too, from the surrounding countryside. Some of them were as young as fourteen. To the youngsters, the smell of the wharves was the smell of fortune and adventure.

In China, there were the strange sights of the city of Canton. Its river was jammed with ferryboats, canal boats, sampans, barges, and junks with eyes painted on their prows. And there were sights just as strange in the cities of India and other nations of the East.

There was money in sailing, too. In the early days of the Salem voyages, each sailor was given space on the ship where the sailor could store goods for trading. These items might be a few kegs of tobacco or some large New England cheeses. Captains could take as much as five tons of goods. Besides their wages, captains were paid from one to eight percent of the profits of the voyage.

The years between the Revolution and the War of 1812 were a great time for Salem. Its warehouses were crammed with the treasures of the East. There, silks from China and coffee from Mocha could be found. The warehouses held painted cloth from India and ivory and gold from the coast of Africa.

Salem's merchants built splendid mansions on Chestnut Street. In their rooms were rare and beautiful things brought from across the sea. Today the mansions still stand. They are reminders of Salem's golden days.

Reading Time _____

Recalling Facts

1. Fishers from Salem caught and traded
   - ❏ a. flounder.
   - ❏ b. codfish.
   - ❏ c. shark.

2. Fish were traded for
   - ❏ a. salt, sugar, or molasses.
   - ❏ b. lumber.
   - ❏ c. gold.

3. To attack British ships during the Revolution, sailors from Salem used American ships called
   - ❏ a. schooners.
   - ❏ b. privateers.
   - ❏ c. barges.

4. Ship captains were paid
   - ❏ a. a flat salary.
   - ❏ b. in goods.
   - ❏ c. wages plus a percentage of the profits.

5. Salem's sailors became wealthy from trading with
   - ❏ a. England.
   - ❏ b. the East.
   - ❏ c. the West Indies.

Understanding Ideas

6. Items from the East that sailors traded could best be described as
   - ❏ a. familiar goods.
   - ❏ b. inexpensive goods.
   - ❏ c. rare and beautiful goods.

7. You can conclude from the article that early sailors were likely to be
   - ❏ a. timid.
   - ❏ b. adventurous.
   - ❏ c. creative.

8. You can conclude that after the Revolutionary War, many of Salem's sailors
   - ❏ a. settled in the East.
   - ❏ b. made money from trading.
   - ❏ c. were lost at sea.

9. You can conclude that the Revolutionary War
   - ❏ a. had no effect on Salem.
   - ❏ b. helped Salem prosper.
   - ❏ c. marked the end of Salem's golden days.

10. The article suggests that Salem
    - ❏ a. has returned to farming.
    - ❏ b. is still a thriving trade center.
    - ❏ c. is no longer a thriving trade center.

18 B   China Fever

On a warm May morning in 1787, the people of Salem, Massachusetts, were hard at work. All at once the boom of a cannon shattered the stillness. People stopped what they were doing. The *Grand Turk* had returned!

Elias Hasket Derby's ship had been gone for 18 months. Its return had been eagerly awaited by the vessel's owner and the wives of the crew. Everyone else in town also awaited its return. All of Salem wanted to see what treasures the first New England ship to sail to Canton, China, would bring home. Everyone in town headed to the wharf.

The *Grand Turk* had sailed to China with a cargo of local goods worth about $32,000. She returned with cargo valued at more than $100,000! People gazed in wonder as bales of silk, boxes of tea, and straw-packed crates of Chinese porcelain were unloaded.

China fever swept Salem. Shops that had stocked only cotton and woolen fabrics added Chinese silk to their wares. Wealthy merchants furnished their homes with hand-carved tables and chairs from the East. They served their guests China's finest tea in delicate cups of Chinese porcelain. Some people even began to wear Chinese-style clothing! Salem would never be the same again!

1. **Recognizing Words in Context**

   Find the word *swept* in the passage. One definition below is a *synonym* for that word; it means the same or almost the same thing. One definition is an *antonym;* it has the opposite or nearly opposite meaning. The other has a completely different meaning. Label the definitions S for *synonym,* A for *antonym,* and D for *different.*

   _____ a. moved slowly
   _____ b. moved quickly
   _____ c. cleared

2. **Distinguishing Fact from Opinion**

   Two of the statements below present *facts,* which can be proved correct. The other statement is an *opinion,* which expresses someone's thoughts or beliefs. Label the statements F for *fact* and O for *opinion.*

   _____ a. The goods from China were wonderful!
   _____ b. The *Grand Turk* had been away for 18 months.
   _____ c. The ship's cargo included tea, silk, and porcelain.

3. Keeping Events in Order

Label the statements below 1, 2, and 3 to show the order in which the events happened.

_____ a. Everyone in Salem headed for the wharf.

_____ b. The *Grand Turk* returned to Salem from Canton, China.

_____ c. Shops added Chinese silk to their wares.

4. Making Correct Inferences

Two of the statements below are correct *inferences,* or reasonable guesses. They are based on information in the passage. The other statement is an incorrect, or faulty, inference. Label the statements C for *correct* inference and F for *faulty* inference.

_____ a. The return of the *Grand Turk* from China marked a turning point in the life of Salem.

_____ b. The people of Salem wanted to move to China.

_____ c. The cargo from China made the owner of the *Grand Turk* wealthy.

5. Understanding Main Ideas

One of the statements below expresses the main idea of the passage. One statement is too general, or too broad. The other explains only part of the passage; it is too narrow. Label the statements M for *main idea*, B for *too broad,* and N for *too narrow.*

_____ a. After 1787, Salem, Massachusetts, became the center of trade with China and other places in the East.

_____ b. The return of the *Grand Turk* from China to Salem with a cargo of silk, tea, and porcelain changed Salem forever.

_____ c. Wealthy merchants served their guests China's finest tea in cups of Chinese porcelain.

Correct Answers, Part A _____

Correct Answers, Part B _____

Total Correct Answers _____

The Great Whales

The great whales are the largest animals that have ever lived. No dinosaur, not even the giant apatosaurus, was as big. Many of the great whales are fifty feet (fifteen meters) long when fully grown, and some are much longer. The blue whale, largest whale of all, often grows from ninety to one hundred feet (twenty-seven to thirty meters) long.

Whales are not fish. They belong to the same group of animals as cows, lions, dogs, and people. Whales are mammals, and like all mammals, they breathe air. They are warm-blooded, give birth to live young, and nurse them with milk. All mammals are hairy, but the dark gray or black skins of whales have almost no hair. Only a few whiskers remain to show that their ancestors were once hairy animals.

These distant ancestors of whales were land animals. Of all the mammals that have returned from the land to live in the sea, such as seals, sea lions, walruses, and manatees, none is as fit as the whale for life in the water.

The great whales are completely streamlined and well suited to water life. Their tapering shape and smooth skin help them move through the water easily. Their bones are soft and spongy, making them light in weight and not very strong for their size. But, since the whale's heavy body is supported by water, a strong skeleton is not as important as it is for a land mammal.

The bones of the whale's short neck are fused together. This gives more support to the huge head, which may make up one-fourth of the entire whale's size. But it also means that the whale cannot turn its head. This may not be much of a loss, since the whale's eyes are small and are set far back. Whales cannot see straight ahead. When they dive below five hundred feet (one hundred fifty-two meters), there is practically no light anyway.

Whales have lost the hind limbs their ancestors once had. Only a few small bones remain inside their bodies near the backbone. The front legs or arms have changed to become flippers, which the whale uses in balancing and steering. Instead of a tail, a whale has a pair of huge, thin, flattened flukes. They are horizontal and move up and down. The flukes are the whale's propeller. The up-and-down wiggle moves the great whale through the water.

Reading Time _____

Recalling Facts

1. The largest whale is the
   - ❑ a. blue whale.
   - ❑ b. gray whale.
   - ❑ c. white whale.

2. Like other mammals, whales
   - ❑ a. have fins.
   - ❑ b. are warm-blooded.
   - ❑ c. do not have hair.

3. Instead of a tail, a whale has
   - ❑ a. legs.
   - ❑ b. flukes.
   - ❑ c. flippers.

4. The whale's heavy body is supported by
   - ❑ a. its skeleton.
   - ❑ b. air pockets.
   - ❑ c. water.

5. Because its neckbones are fused, the whale
   - ❑ a. can only see what is directly in front of it.
   - ❑ b. cannot see in the dark.
   - ❑ c. cannot turn its head.

Understanding Ideas

6. You can conclude from the article that whales
   - ❑ a. can stay underwater longer than any other mammal.
   - ❑ b. must surface in order to breathe.
   - ❑ c. breathe by finding underwater air pockets.

7. If a whale lived on land, it is likely that
   - ❑ a. its skeleton would not support its weight.
   - ❑ b. it would weigh more than it does in the water.
   - ❑ c. its body would be larger.

8. You can conclude that a whale's sense of sight is
   - ❑ a. very important.
   - ❑ b. more important than hearing.
   - ❑ c. not very important.

9. You can conclude that in order to live in the water, the whale
   - ❑ a. grew larger in size.
   - ❑ b. had to learn to swim.
   - ❑ c. changed physically.

10. It is likely that whales will
    - ❑ a. remain water mammals.
    - ❑ b. return to land once again.
    - ❑ c. eventually become fish.

The young whale had followed a school of fish upward toward the bottom of a fishing trawler floating on the surface. Suddenly, she became entangled in a fishing net! The whale twisted and turned to no avail. She could not free herself. The harder she struggled, the more entangled she became. At long last, the net ripped free, but part of it remained wrapped around the whale's mouth and tail.

Weeks passed. Dragging the heavy net greatly tired the whale. She could barely open her mouth to eat. She became thinner and weaker. Finally, she could no longer swim to the surface to breathe. If she could not get to the surface for air, she would drown. Other whales gathered around and pushed her up into the air.

Then one day the whales heard the roar of boat engines. As the boat neared the whales, the engines stopped. Two rafts were lowered into the sea, and people climbed into them. The other whales quickly swam away—but not the young whale wrapped in a net. The rafts and boat circled her, and the people attached floats to pieces of the net that entangled her. The floats held her in place as hands reached down and began cutting the net. Soon, the last cords were cut, and the net fell away. The whale was free! She blew a spout from her blowhole as if to say "thank you" and swam off.

1. Recognizing Words in Context

Find the word *circled* in the passage. One definition below is a *synonym* for that word; it means the same or almost the same thing. One definition is an *antonym;* it has the opposite or nearly opposite meaning. The other has a completely different meaning. Label the definitions S for *synonym,* A for *antonym,* and D for *different.*

_____ a. went around

_____ b. surrounded

_____ c. left

2. Distinguishing Fact from Opinion

Two of the statements below present *facts,* which can be proved correct. The other statement is an *opinion,* which expresses someone's thoughts or beliefs. Label the statements F for *fact* and O for *opinion.*

_____ a. Fishers should not be allowed to use nets where whales are swimming.

_____ b. The whale became entangled in a fishing net.

_____ c. She grew thinner and weaker.

3. Keeping Events in Order

Label the statements below 1, 2, and 3 to show the order in which the events happened.

_____ a. People cut away the net and freed the whale.

_____ b. The net made it hard for the whale to open her mouth.

_____ c. The whale became thinner and weaker.

4. Making Correct Inferences

Two of the statements below are correct *inferences,* or reasonable guesses. They are based on information in the passage. The other statement is an incorrect, or faulty, inference. Label the statements C for *correct* inference and F for *faulty* inference.

_____ a. If the net had not been cut away, the whale would have died.

_____ b. The other whales knew they had to help the whale get to the surface to breathe.

_____ c. All whales eat fish.

5. Understanding Main Ideas

One of the statements below expresses the main idea of the passage. One statement is too general, or too broad. The other explains only part of the passage; it is too narrow. Label the statements M for *main idea,* B for *too broad,* and N for *too narrow.*

_____ a. Other whales gathered around the whale and pushed her to the surface so that she could breathe.

_____ b. A whale caught in a fishing net is saved when people cut the net away and free her.

_____ c. Whales are mammals and, like all mammals, they breathe air.

Correct Answers, Part A _____

Correct Answers, Part B _____

Total Correct Answers _____

A Pet Parakeet

Few pets are as popular as parakeets, also called budgies. These are small parrots native to tropical regions. The beautifully colored little bird is a fine pet for shut-ins and people who live in apartments. Its friendliness and playfulness make it a lively companion.

With patience, you can teach almost any parakeet to talk. Usually a young parakeet is easier to train than a mature bird. When you bring your budgie home, let it stay in its cage from one to two weeks until you see that it is used to its new surroundings and to you.

At first, your pet may not be able to find the food cup. Spread seed liberally among the gravel on the floor of the cage. Feed your budgie once a day. When it learns to eat from the cup, empty the waste hulls daily. Be sure it has grit. It also likes little extras in its treat cup, such as millet seed, a bit of green or apple, and finely chopped egg.

When a budgie becomes tame in its cage, you can finger train it. You may start by talking quietly to it as you slowly and repeatedly put your hand in its cage, near the bottom. It will come to sit on your finger. Then you can train it to stay on a playpen, a wood tray with sides raised to keep gravel from spilling. You can fit it with a variety of toys, such as bells, ladders, seesaw, and trapeze.

To teach your bird to talk, begin training it as soon as it is cage-tame. A budgie learns faster when it is the only bird. Some people cover the cage while they speak to the bird so that it will concentrate on the voice. A budgie seems to find words starting with *p* and *b* the easiest to learn. Stand at the cage and, in your normal tone, say clearly a simple phrase such as "pretty Bill." Repeat several times a day, if possible, or at least five minutes each morning and night. Only when your pet has learned that one phrase should you teach it another.

Some budgies talk after two months of training. Others may take six months. Many people use parakeet recordings for teaching. Others prefer to train by their own voices, for the bird imitates the tone of its trainer. Some parakeets learn hundreds of words.

Reading Time _____

Recalling Facts

1. Budgie is another name for a
   - ❏ a. parrot.
   - ❏ b. parakeet.
   - ❏ c. mature bird.

2. When you bring your parakeet home, at first you should
   - ❏ a. finger train it.
   - ❏ b. let it explore your home.
   - ❏ c. let it stay in its cage.

3. A parakeet should be fed
   - ❏ a. once a day.
   - ❏ b. twice a day.
   - ❏ c. three times a day.

4. You can teach your bird to talk
   - ❏ a. when it is mature.
   - ❏ b. as soon as it is cage-tame.
   - ❏ c. as soon as you bring it home.

5. Parakeets easily learn words starting with
   - ❏ a. *s* and *t*.
   - ❏ b. *b* and *c*.
   - ❏ c. *p* and *b*.

Understanding Ideas

6. The article suggests that parakeets make
   - ❏ a. interesting pets.
   - ❏ b. poor pets.
   - ❏ c. dangerous pets.

7. You can conclude from the article that parakeets like
   - ❏ a. a varied diet.
   - ❏ b. the same food every day.
   - ❏ c. the same food that people eat.

8. You can conclude that it is best to train a parakeet
   - ❏ a. all at once.
   - ❏ b. once a week.
   - ❏ c. in stages.

9. Parakeets probably learn to talk by
   - ❏ a. reading lips.
   - ❏ b. imitating sounds.
   - ❏ c. making up sounds.

10. You can conclude that a parakeet learns faster when it
    - ❏ a. is rewarded with food.
    - ❏ b. can learn from other birds.
    - ❏ c. is not distracted.

Jake was excited when he brought his new parakeet home. He was going to teach his bird to speak. Jake decided that the first words he would teach the bird were "Pretty boy."

Every morning before school, Jake stood in front of the bird's cage repeating the words, "Pretty boy. Pretty boy." He always said the same words over and over again for five minutes straight. When he came home from school, he did it again. "Pretty boy. Pretty boy," he repeated for five minutes. The parakeet twittered and made parakeet noises, but it never said a word.

"Quit it, Jake!" his sister Serina told him. "You're driving me crazy!"

"The pet shop owner said that in order to get a parakeet to talk, you have to say the same thing over and over," Jake told Serina. "That's what I'm doing."

A week later, Jake was still saying, "Pretty boy. Pretty boy." The parakeet was still just twittering and making parakeet noises. By now, everyone in the family was saying, "Quit it, Jake!" Jake just ignored them. He was determined to get the bird to talk.

Then finally, the parakeet spoke!

"Pretty boy. Pretty boy," Jake was saying to the bird.

"Quit it, Jake!" the parakeet said clearly.

1. Recognizing Words in Context

Find the word *straight* in the passage. One definition below is a *synonym* for that word; it means the same or almost the same thing. One definition is an *antonym;* it has the opposite or nearly opposite meaning. The other has a completely different meaning. Label the definitions S for *synonym,* A for *antonym,* and D for *different*.

_____ a. continuously

_____ b. occasionally

_____ c. unbending

2. Distinguishing Fact from Opinion

Two of the statements below present *facts,* which can be proved correct. The other statement is an *opinion,* which expresses someone's thoughts or beliefs. Label the statements F for *fact* and O for *opinion*.

_____ a. Jake had been told to repeat the same thing to the parakeet over and over.

_____ b. Jake kept saying, "Pretty boy."

_____ c. Jake was driving his sister Serina crazy.

3. Keeping Events in Order

Label the statements below 1, 2, and 3 to show the order in which the events happened.

_____ a. Jake kept repeating "Pretty boy" to his parakeet.

_____ b. Jake's sister Serina told him, "Quit it, Jake."

_____ c. The parakeet said, "Quit it, Jake."

4. Making Correct Inferences

Two of the statements below are correct *inferences*, or reasonable guesses. They are based on information in the passage. The other statement is an incorrect, or faulty, inference. Label the statements C for *correct* inference and F for *faulty* inference.

_____ a. The parakeet learned to say "Quit it, Jake," from hearing family members say it.

_____ b. Listening to Jake say "Pretty boy" over and over annoyed other family members.

_____ c. The parakeet did not want to say "Pretty boy."

5. Understanding Main Ideas

One of the statements below expresses the main idea of the passage. One statement is too general, or too broad. The other explains only part of the passage; it is too narrow. Label the statements M for *main idea*, B for *too broad*, and N for *too narrow*.

_____ a. Like other members of the parrot family, parakeets can be trained to speak.

_____ b. Jake tried to teach his parakeet to say "Pretty boy," but what the bird finally said was "Quit it, Jake!"

_____ c. Jake repeated "Pretty boy" to his parakeet every morning and afternoon.

Correct Answers, Part A _____

Correct Answers, Part B _____

Total Correct Answers _____

A Desert Fox

When you think of the desert, you may think of thirst. But thirst is not the only problem facing those who live in deserts. Water alone will not sustain life. For animals in the desert, hunger and the search for food consume a major part of their daily lives. Because the desert can be a hostile place, animals living there have adapted in special ways that help them find food. One such animal is the little kit fox.

The kit fox is about the size and weight of a large house cat. It resembles its distant cousin, the gray fox. Both have thick coats and bushy tails. But the fur of the kit fox is buff yellow or gray, with black-tipped hairs. It becomes a perfect disguise for slipping around in the desert moonlight. The kit fox ranges over nearly the whole western desert in the United States. But it is rarely seen, and never in daylight. Anyone who spends time in the desert may, from time to time, catch a glimpse of the kit fox and find its tracks in the sand.

Kit foxes are unafraid and rather curious about people, yet they remain shy. They live underground in burrows that may extend up to eight feet (2.4 meters). There the kit fox spends the hot part of each day. There once a year the young, called kittens, are born. Usually kit foxes have four or five kittens in a litter.

The kit fox feeds on any small animals it can find, but its favorite is the kangaroo rat. The kangaroo rat has been called the "staff of life" for the kit fox. Rat burrows that have been dug open by foxes can be found in sandy areas. The kit foxes eat wood rats, pocket mice, small birds, lizards, and insects, too.

Smells vanish quickly in dry desert winds. Instead of a keen sense of smell, the successful hunter needs acute hearing. The kit fox's ears are much larger in proportion to its size than the ears of other foxes. They are broad and pointed. Its ears can be moved independently, allowing the kit fox to listen in two directions at once. At the slightest sound, its ears twitch, listening for the direction of prey. Then the animal turns toward the sound, moving swiftly on its short, sturdy legs. The kit fox's ears are a helpful adaptation to desert life.

Reading Time _____

Recalling Facts

1. In size, a kit fox resembles a
   - ❏ a. large house cat.
   - ❏ b. kangaroo rat.
   - ❏ c. pocket mouse.

2. To a kit fox, people are
   - ❏ a. frightening.
   - ❏ b. objects of curiosity.
   - ❏ c. natural enemies.

3. A kit fox's diet consists mostly of
   - ❏ a. plants.
   - ❏ b. insects.
   - ❏ c. small animals.

4. A desert hunter's most important sense is
   - ❏ a. sight.
   - ❏ b. hearing.
   - ❏ c. smell.

5. A distinctive characteristic of the kit fox is its
   - ❏ a. ears.
   - ❏ b. nose.
   - ❏ c. head.

Understanding Ideas

6. You can conclude from the article that the kit fox is
   - ❏ a. smaller than other foxes.
   - ❏ b. larger than other foxes.
   - ❏ c. about the same size as other foxes.

7. It is likely that the kit fox
   - ❏ a. will learn to fear people.
   - ❏ b. has not been harmed by people.
   - ❏ c. will learn to trust people.

8. You can conclude that adaptations made by animals
   - ❏ a. are more pronounced in the desert.
   - ❏ b. vary according to where they live.
   - ❏ c. are usually changes in coloring.

9. It is likely that a kit fox's shyness
   - ❏ a. helps it find food.
   - ❏ b. allows it to hear better.
   - ❏ c. protects it from its enemies.

10. You can conclude that a kit fox does most of its hunting
   - ❏ a. at night.
   - ❏ b. during the afternoon.
   - ❏ c. in the morning.

As night falls on the desert, the kit fox emerges from her burrow. She has slept all day, but now she is ready to hunt.

Prowling about, she sees something moving and begins creeping up on it. It is a jackrabbit eating a juicy cactus stem. Just as the fox is about to spring, some tiny sound or movement betrays her. She pounces, but her prey bounds off.

The kit fox settles her fur and starts out again. Suddenly, her hackles rise. There is a whiff of coyote on the breeze. She scurries away just in time to avoid becoming a meal herself.

The fox's sharp ears catch a scratching sound, and she snaps up a scorpion, crunching it down before it can bite her. Now the edge is off her hunger, but she is not ready to return to her burrow. Moving in a wide circle, she hears a kangaroo rat munching on a mesquite pod. She inches toward it and pounces, trapping the rat between her paws. She bites its neck hard, killing it quickly. Then she starts back to her burrow, carrying her prize. It will make a fine meal to carry her through the coming day.

1. **Recognizing Words in Context**

   Find the word *edge* in the passage. One definition below is a *synonym* for that word; it means the same or almost the same thing. One definition is an *antonym;* it has the opposite or nearly opposite meaning. The other has a completely different meaning. Label the definitions S for *synonym*, A for *antonym*, and D for *different*.

   _____ a. sharpness

   _____ b. border

   _____ c. dullness

2. **Distinguishing Fact from Opinion**

   Two of the statements below present *facts*, which can be proved correct. The other statement is an *opinion,* which expresses someone's thoughts or beliefs. Label the statements F for *fact* and O for *opinion*.

   _____ a. The kit fox slept all day and emerged from her burrow at night.

   _____ b. The kangaroo rat will make a fine meal.

   _____ c. The kit fox lives in a burrow.

3. Keeping Events in Order

Label the statements below 1, 2, and 3 to show the order in which the events happened.

_____ a. The fox catches the scent of a coyote.

_____ b. The fox fails to catch a jackrabbit.

_____ c. The fox catches a kangaroo rat.

4. Making Correct Inferences

Two of the statements below are correct *inferences,* or reasonable guesses. They are based on information in the passage. The other statement is an incorrect, or faulty, inference. Label the statements C for *correct* inference and F for *faulty* inference.

_____ a. Kit foxes prey on different kinds of animals.

_____ b. Kit foxes can fall prey to other desert creatures.

_____ c. Kit foxes are not good hunters.

5. Understanding Main Ideas

One of the statements below expresses the main idea of the passage. One statement is too general, or too broad. The other explains only part of the passage; it is too narrow. Label the statements M for *main idea,* B for *too broad,* and N for *too narrow.*

_____ a. Hunger and the search for food consume a major part of the daily lives of desert animals such as the kit fox.

_____ b. The kit fox just misses catching a jackrabbit, which bounds away as she is about to pounce.

_____ c. A kit fox emerges from her burrow at night to hunt for food and is successful.

Correct Answers, Part A _____

Correct Answers, Part B _____

Total Correct Answers _____

There are eight planets besides Earth in the sun's family. The word *planet* means "wanderer." When the people of ancient times studied the sky, they gave names to the groups of stars they saw. They learned to know the stars that made up each group. They saw some "stars," however, that did not stay in any one group. These "stars" came to be called wanderers, or planets. Finally, people realized that these "stars" were not stars at all, but bodies, like Earth, that keep traveling around the sun. They seem to wander from star group to star group because of their journeys around the sun.

Planets look to people like stars, but they are really very different. Stars are very, very hot. They shine with their own light. Planets do not shine with their own light. They shine only because the sun is shining on them. Moonlight, as most people know, is secondhand sunlight. The moon merely reflects the light that shines on it from the sun. The light from planets is secondhand sunlight, too.

Of the eight other planets, only five can be seen with the naked eye. People of ancient times knew of only five "wandering stars." The other planets were not discovered until after telescopes were invented. The planets that are visible without a telescope are Mercury, Venus, Mars, Jupiter, and Saturn. The others are Uranus, Neptune, and Pluto.

The path of a planet is called its orbit. The planets keep traveling their same orbits around the sun century after century. They do not stray from their path because the sun is pulling them with so much force that they cannot escape. Scientists call the power with which the sun is pulling the planets the force of gravitation. Often this force is called gravity for short.

It would seem that if the sun is pulling the planets with so much force, the planets would fall into the sun. They do not because they are moving too fast. Each planet moves with a speed that just balances the pull of the sun. The outer planets move more slowly than those closer to the sun.

Many of the planets have moons that travel around them as they travel around the sun. Earth has one moon. Mercury, Venus, and Pluto have none. Jupiter, in contrast, has twelve moons. Mars and Neptune have two. Uranus has five, and Saturn has nine.

Reading Time _____

Recalling Facts

1. The sun's family includes
   - ❏ a. eight planets.
   - ❏ b. nine planets.
   - ❏ c. ten planets.

2. In the night sky, planets shine
   - ❏ a. with their own light.
   - ❏ b. because of the moonlight.
   - ❏ c. with reflected light.

3. A planet that was discovered after the invention of the telescope is
   - ❏ a. Venus.
   - ❏ b. Jupiter.
   - ❏ c. Neptune.

4. Planets stay in their orbits around the sun because of
   - ❏ a. reflection.
   - ❏ b. gravity.
   - ❏ c. secondhand sunlight.

5. Each planet moves with a speed that
   - ❏ a. just balances the sun's pull.
   - ❏ b. changes daily.
   - ❏ c. varies with the seasons.

Understanding Ideas

6. You can conclude from the article that the planets that can be seen with the naked eye move
   - ❏ a. faster than those that cannot.
   - ❏ b. slower than those that cannot.
   - ❏ c. both faster and slower than those that cannot.

7. You can conclude that compared to a star, a planet is
   - ❏ a. hotter.
   - ❏ b. cooler.
   - ❏ c. about the same temperature.

8. The article suggests that studying the skies
   - ❏ a. is no longer useful.
   - ❏ b. began with the invention of the telescope.
   - ❏ c. is an ancient pastime.

9. You can conclude that if the planets were to reduce their speed, they would
   - ❏ a. be pulled into the sun.
   - ❏ b. fall into the universe.
   - ❏ c. bump into each other.

10. You can conclude that without the sun's light, Earth would
   - ❏ a. receive light from the moon.
   - ❏ b. not exist.
   - ❏ c. be cold and dark.

On July 6, 1997, the first roving vehicle ever to explore another planet rolled onto the surface of Mars. Scientists at the Jet Propulsion Laboratory in Pasadena, California, whooped with joy. Called Sojourner, the foot-high (30-cm-high) robot was equipped with a 3-D camera. It also had an instrument that could chemically analyze the Martian surface.

Sojourner rolled down the ramp from Pathfinder. The Pathfinder was the lander that carried Sojourner to Mars. Sojourner traveled about four inches (10 cm). It stopped to take soil samples. Then it slowly moved on. The rover shot hundreds of pictures and sent them back to Earth. Pathfinder scientists gave playful nicknames to the rocks Sojourner encountered. They named many after cartoon characters—Barnacle Bill, Yogi, Scooby Doo, Flat Top, Boo Boo. Scientists were thrilled with the information the rover provided.

Today Mars is a dry, cold, windy desert. Once, though, water flooded the plain where Pathfinder landed. Scientists think the floodwaters may have been hundreds of feet (meters) deep. Today, the air is too thin and the atmospheric pressure too low for Mars to have surface water. Long ago, though, the atmosphere was thicker and the climate much warmer. Then it could have had water. Sojourner has given scientists a whole new image of the sun's fourth planet.

1. **Recognizing Words in Context**

   Find the word *plain* in the passage. One definition below is a *synonym* for that word; it means the same or almost the same thing. One definition is an *antonym;* it has the opposite or nearly opposite meaning. The other has a completely different meaning. Label the definitions S for *synonym,* A for *antonym,* and D for *different.*

   _____ a. flat land

   _____ b. undecorated

   _____ c. mountain

2. **Distinguishing Fact from Opinion**

   Two of the statements below present *facts,* which can be proved correct. The other statement is an *opinion,* which expresses someone's thoughts or beliefs. Label the statements F for *fact* and O for *opinion.*

   _____ a. Sojourner was equipped with a 3-D camera.

   _____ b. Sojourner's information about Mars is the most important discovery ever made about space.

   _____ c. Scientists gave the Martian rocks names, such as Scooby Doo and Boo Boo.

3. Keeping Events in Order

Two of the statements below describe events that happened at the same time. The other statement describes an event that happened before or after those events. Label them S for *same time*, B for *before*, and A for *after*.

_____ a. Pathfinder carried Sojourner to Mars.

_____ b. Sojourner rolled down the ramp from Pathfinder and onto the Martian surface.

_____ c. Scientists at the Jet Propulsion Laboratory whooped with joy.

4. Making Correct Inferences

Two of the statements below are correct *inferences*, or reasonable guesses. They are based on information in the passage. The other statement is an incorrect, or faulty, inference. Label the statements C for *correct* inference and F for *faulty* inference.

_____ a. Scientists considered Sojourner's mission a great success.

_____ b. The water that flooded the plain must still be on Mars somewhere.

_____ c. Sojourner's findings gave scientists important new information about Mars.

5. Understanding Main Ideas

One of the statements below expresses the main idea of the passage. One statement is too general, or too broad. The other explains only part of the passage; it is too narrow. Label the statements M for *main idea*, B for *too broad*, and N for *too narrow*.

_____ a. Sojourner, a robot explorer that landed on Mars in July 1997, sent back information about great floods that had covered Mars long ago.

_____ b. The climate of Mars has changed dramatically over billions of years.

_____ c. Sojourner sent back hundreds of pictures of Mars.

Correct Answers, Part A _____

Correct Answers, Part B _____

Total Correct Answers _____

Every boy of noble birth had to pass through many years of training before he could become a knight. It began when he was young, perhaps not more than seven years old. Sometimes a boy received his training at home, but more often he went to live at the castle of some lord of renown and wealth. Every important noble had several young lads living as pages in his castle.

The pages helped the ladies of the castle in every way they could. From them, the pages learned many things. One lady would take a special interest in each page. She would teach him how to sing and dance. She taught him how to compose music and perhaps play the harp. The lady told him stories of knights and taught him how to read. In their spare time, the pages played games, and each had daily exercise in the castle yard.

For seven years or more, a boy lived at the castle as a page. Then he became a squire. A squire served his lord in many ways. He polished armor, keeping it bright and shining. He helped care for horses. A squire waited upon his lord at mealtime, carrying water, carving meat, and filling his cup when it was empty. A squire rode with his lord to tournaments and to battle, carrying his shield and weapons. If his lord was unhorsed in a tournament, the squire rushed in and remounted him. If his lord was wounded in battle, the squire carried him to a place of safety and helped care for his wounds.

The squire practiced in the castle yard. He learned to be at home on a horse's back and to hold his lance correctly. He practiced managing his shield while his horse was charging.

Always a squire was looking forward to the time when he would become a knight. Sometimes this took place simply on the battlefield when a squire had shown particular bravery in helping save his lord's life in time of danger. But ordinarily the knighting was done at the castle and was accompanied by a solemn religious ceremony.

Knights were guided by the ideals of chivalry. The knight was expected to be loyal to the church and to his overlord. He was always to speak the truth and to stand up for what was right. Knighthood demanded a high standard of conduct and integrity.

Reading Time _____

Recalling Facts

1. Boys in training to become knights first lived in castles as
   - ❑ a. squires.
   - ❑ b. nobles.
   - ❑ c. pages.

2. Among the duties of a squire was
   - ❑ a. polishing armor.
   - ❑ b. learning to read.
   - ❑ c. composing music.

3. Knights were expected to
   - ❑ a. teach the pages.
   - ❑ b. be loyal to their church.
   - ❑ c. care for the lord's horse.

4. Knights were guided by the ideals of
   - ❑ a. poetry.
   - ❑ b. swordsmanship.
   - ❑ c. chivalry.

5. Knighting was usually accompanied by
   - ❑ a. parades.
   - ❑ b. religious ceremonies.
   - ❑ c. political speeches.

Understanding Ideas

6. You can conclude from the article that boys of noble birth
   - ❑ a. all wanted to become knights.
   - ❑ b. did not all become knights.
   - ❑ c. had to become knights.

7. A knight in training owed his first duty to
   - ❑ a. the church.
   - ❑ b. his family.
   - ❑ c. his lord.

8. You can conclude that a knight was known for his
   - ❑ a. sense of honor.
   - ❑ b. sense of humor.
   - ❑ c. learning.

9. A good squire had to be
   - ❑ a. courageous.
   - ❑ b. scholarly.
   - ❑ c. wealthy.

10. You can conclude that in early times horses in battle were
    - ❑ a. rare.
    - ❑ b. commonplace.
    - ❑ c. unsuitable.

Hawking Lessons

We go hawking on Tuesdays, after our lessons with Brother Geoffrey from the abbey. I have a kestrel named Linnea that I have trained from a nestling. She now comes instantly when I whistle.

First, we taught Linnea to come to my glove. I would hold a piece of meat. Hob, the falconer, then released Linnea to fly to me. Gradually, Hob increased his distance. We kept Linnea on a long lead so that she could not fly away. When she began coming to me regularly, I worked her with a lure—a dead pigeon on a rope. I tossed and twirled the lure in the air so that it looked like the pigeon was flying. Linnea flew to the lure and caught it in her talons. Soon she was ready to try real game.

Today I was walking with Linnea on my glove when a grouse suddenly flew up in front of us. I quickly removed Linnea's hood and released her. She took the grouse in midair! It was a thrilling sight. The bells on Linnea's legs would help me find her if I should lose her in the tall grass, but she came to me right away. Naturally, I rewarded her with a bit of fresh grouse.

1. Recognizing Words in Context

Find the word *bit* in the passage. One definition below is a *synonym* for that word; it means the same or almost the same thing. One definition is an *antonym;* it has the opposite or nearly opposite meaning. The other has a completely different meaning. Label the definitions S for *synonym,* A for *antonym,* and D for *different.*

_____ a. large chunk

_____ b. seized

_____ c. small piece

2. Distinguishing Fact from Opinion

Two of the statements below present *facts,* which can be proved correct. The other statement is an *opinion,* which expresses someone's thoughts or beliefs. Label the statements F for *fact* and O for *opinion.*

_____ a. Seeing the kestrel take the grouse was thrilling.

_____ b. The kestrel caught a grouse in midair.

_____ c. The narrator trained a kestrel.

3. Keeping Events in Order

Two of the statements below describe events that happened at the same time. The other statement describes an event that happened before or after those events. Label them S for *same time*, B for *before*, and A for *after*.

_____ a. The falconer releases the hawk.

_____ b. The narrator twirls a lure in the air.

_____ c. The narrator holds a piece of meat in his gloved hand.

4. Making Correct Inferences

Two of the statements below are correct *inferences*, or reasonable guesses. They are based on information in the passage. The other statement is an incorrect, or faulty, inference. Label the statements C for *correct* inference and F for *faulty* inference.

_____ a. Hawking was an important part of the narrator's education.

_____ b. Hawks become gentle with training.

_____ c. Training a hawk requires patience and persistence.

5. Understanding Main Ideas

One of the statements below expresses the main idea of the passage. One statement is too general, or too broad. The other explains only part of the passage; it is too narrow. Label the statements M for *main idea*, B for *too broad*, and N for *too narrow*.

_____ a. The kestrel was trained to catch game in flight through the use of a lure.

_____ b. Hawking is a sport with a long history.

_____ c. A boy works with a falconer to train a kestrel to catch game and is rewarded when it performs perfectly in the field.

Correct Answers, Part A _____

Correct Answers, Part B _____

Total Correct Answers _____

John Ericsson, Inventor

John Ericsson was born in Sweden when Thomas Jefferson was president of the United States. He grew up among the woods and lakes of Sweden. He did not attend public school. Three days a week, a tutor came to John's home to teach him and his brothers. They were taught whatever their parents thought they should learn.

John Ericsson learned quickly, especially in drawing. But he was most interested in his father's iron mines and the machinery in them. When the tutor was not at the house, John went to the mines. He would ask the miners how things worked. Afterward he would go home and build models of the mine machinery. He used cords and pieces of wood to make his models.

When John was a teen-ager, a canal was being built all the way across Sweden. The Swedish government wanted to set up a corps of engineers. Their job would be to run the canal after it was finished. John's father had him appointed as a cadet engineer. John and the other cadets attended classes in engineering. Senior engineers taught them algebra, geometry, and drawing.

In 1826, John went to London. Steam engines had become practical only a few years before. John's engineering studies helped him understand these new engines. He often found ways to improve the engines, because ideas came to him as he was working on them.

Ericsson made over twenty inventions, mostly engines or parts of engines in England. As a result, he became known as one of the best engineers in England. His main invention was the screw propeller. At this time, all steamships were pushed through the water by enormous paddle wheels, one on each side of the vessel. Between them, in the middle of the ship, the engines were placed.

This seemed a very poor system to John. The big paddle wheels were always breaking against floating objects. The huge wheels could turn only very slowly. Ericsson believed that all this could be done away with if the ship were driven by a large screw. A screw propeller would be much smaller and take less power for the same speed.

Ericsson was busy with other things. It took him four years to work out the shape of the blades. A ship using the propeller was tried out in 1839. It was such a success that soon everybody was building ships with screw propellers.

Reading Time _____

Recalling Facts

1. John Ericsson was born in
   - ❏ a. England.
   - ❏ b. Sweden.
   - ❏ c. the United States.

2. As a young student, Ericsson did very well in
   - ❏ a. drawing.
   - ❏ b. algebra.
   - ❏ c. English.

3. Ericsson was especially curious about
   - ❏ a. plants and animals.
   - ❏ b. history.
   - ❏ c. machines.

4. Ericsson's inventions in England dealt with
   - ❏ a. engines.
   - ❏ b. sailboats.
   - ❏ c. mining equipment.

5. Ericsson's main invention was the
   - ❏ a. paddle wheel.
   - ❏ b. screw propeller.
   - ❏ c. steamship.

Understanding Ideas

6. You can conclude from the article that good engineers are likely to be
   - ❏ a. curious.
   - ❏ b. stubborn.
   - ❏ c. humorous.

7. Ericsson was talented at
   - ❏ a. writing short stories.
   - ❏ b. making things.
   - ❏ c. sports.

8. Ericsson's inventions most likely resulted from his desire to
   - ❏ a. improve people's daily lives.
   - ❏ b. improve people's minds.
   - ❏ c. make things work better.

9. You can conclude that if Ericsson lived today, he would probably be
   - ❏ a. a historian.
   - ❏ b. an artist.
   - ❏ c. an inventor.

10. You can conclude that Ericsson was a successful inventor because he
    - ❏ a. liked to keep busy.
    - ❏ b. worked slowly.
    - ❏ c. worked at problems until he solved them.

24 B   Pour on the Lard!

Mrs. Gray boarded the steamboat headed for New Orleans. She was taking barrels of lard to markets in New Orleans. Her friends had warned her about the dangers of steamboat travel. One of the worst dangers, they said, was when steamboat captains raced their boats. Boilers used to generate the steam that power the boats could explode when overstoked.

As the steamboat set off, Mrs. Gray approached the captain. "Captain," she said, "I want you to promise me that you will not race this boat."

"I never race," he swore, "at least, hardly ever."

The boat steamed peacefully downriver. Then another boat drew alongside. Both boats speeded up. Black smoke poured out of the rival boat's stacks as it pulled ahead.

"Captain! Are you racing that boat?" Mrs. Gray cried.

"Yes, Ma'am, and we're losing," he answered. "See that black smoke? They're putting oil on their wood to make it burn hotter. We can't get our boilers hot enough to beat it on wood alone."

Mrs. Gray wasn't one to lose a challenge. "Get my lard, Captain!" Mrs. Gray shouted. "Put it on the wood, and heat up your boilers!"

With the lard-soaked wood, the fires leaped up. The steamboat's wheels turned faster and faster. As the boat passed its rival, Mrs. Gray cheered and shook her fist at the loser!

1. **Recognizing Words in Context**

   Find the word *pulled* in the passage. One definition below is a *synonym* for that word; it means the same or almost the same thing. One definition is an *antonym;* it has the opposite or nearly opposite meaning. The other has a completely different meaning. Label the definitions S for *synonym*, A for *antonym,* and D for *different.*

   _____ a. moved
   _____ b. dragged
   _____ c. stopped

2. **Distinguishing Fact from Opinion**

   Two of the statements below present *facts,* which can be proved correct. The other statement is an *opinion,* which expresses someone's thoughts or beliefs. Label the statements F for *fact* and O for *opinion.*

   _____ a. Mrs. Gray asked the captain to promise not to race his boat.
   _____ b. One of the worst dangers of steamboat travel was a race.
   _____ c. Oil poured on wood made the wood burn hotter.

3. Keeping Events in Order

Two of the statements below describe events that happened at the same time. The other statement describes an event that happened before or after those events. Label them S for *same time*, B for *before*, and A for *after*.

_____ a. The steamboat Mrs. Gray was on passed its rival.

_____ b. Mrs. Gray told the captain to pour her lard on the wood.

_____ c. Mrs. Gray cheered and shook her fist at the rival boat.

4. Making Correct Inferences

Two of the statements below are correct *inferences,* or reasonable guesses. They are based on information in the passage. The other statement is an incorrect, or faulty, inference. Label the statements C for *correct* inference and F for *faulty* inference.

_____ a. Mrs. Gray had been hoping for a boat race all along.

_____ b. The lard made the wood burn hotter.

_____ c. The hotter the fire in the boilers, the faster the boat could go.

5. Understanding Main Ideas

One of the statements below expresses the main idea of the passage. One statement is too general, or too broad. The other explains only part of the passage; it is too narrow. Label the statements M for *main idea,* B for *too broad,* and N for *too narrow.*

_____ a. The rival steamboat's crew had poured oil on wood to make it burn hotter.

_____ b. Steamboats were fueled by wood-burning boilers.

_____ c. When the steamboat was losing a race, Mrs. Gray gave her lard to be used as fuel so that her boat would win.

Correct Answers, Part A _____

Correct Answers, Part B _____

Total Correct Answers _____

The Lions of Africa

On the plains of Africa, lions continue to thrive. They do their best hunting on the plateaus of eastern Africa and in the vast grasslands of the south. Their roar is the most fear-inspiring voice of the grasslands. Lions live in rocky dens, in thorn-tree thickets, or in tall grasses at the edges of streams.

Except for the tiger, the lion is the largest member of the cat family. Its body is covered with short yellow-brown hair. A coarse mane grows on the male's head, neck, and shoulders. The female lacks a mane. As a rule, she is more slender and about a foot (30 centimeters) shorter than the male.

Much of the hunting is done by the female. Colored like sun-dried grass, the lion can slip unseen across the plains. Its jaws are hinged so that it can open its mouth wide enough to kill a zebra or a medium-sized antelope with one bite.

Lions usually hunt at night. The lion often hides beside a trail leading to a water hole and then pounces upon the shoulder or flank of a passing animal. It drives its claws deep into the flesh and kills its victim with a stabbing and crunching bite on the throat or the back of the neck. When stalking a herd, the lion creeps up from the side toward which the wind is blowing, taking advantage of cover until the moment of the last quick rush.

A pride of 4 to 12 lions sometimes hunts together, working as a team. The males roar loudly to scare up the game, while the females lie in wait along the trails to pounce on the rushing animals. After the females make a kill, the males come to eat.

Lions usually pair for life. About 16 weeks after mating time, the young (from two to four) are born in a private spot chosen by the mother. She guards her offspring jealously and does not permit even the male to approach. He is prone by instinct to kill his own young.

Usually lions avoid humans. However, old ones too slow to catch game may become man-eaters. From time to time, a young lion that gets a taste of human blood may continue to kill humans.

Since the days of the Roman Empire, lions have been caged for circuses and zoos. Most of those that are seen today have been born in captivity.

Reading Time _____

Recalling Facts

1. Compared to other members of the cat family, the lion is
   - ❑ a. small.
   - ❑ b. the largest.
   - ❑ c. the second largest.

2. Lions usually hunt
   - ❑ a. at sunrise.
   - ❑ b. during the day.
   - ❑ c. at night.

3. A group of lions is called a
   - ❑ a. herd.
   - ❑ b. pride.
   - ❑ c. flock.

4. Young lions are in danger from
   - ❑ a. the mother lion.
   - ❑ b. the father lion.
   - ❑ c. both parents.

5. Most lions seen today are born in
   - ❑ a. captivity.
   - ❑ b. Africa.
   - ❑ c. the wild.

Understanding Ideas

6. You can conclude from the article that a lion's coloring
   - ❑ a. changes with the seasons.
   - ❑ b. varies according to where it lives.
   - ❑ c. helps it hide from its prey.

7. It is likely that lions stalk their prey against the wind in order to
   - ❑ a. reduce the sound of their approach.
   - ❑ b. keep their scent from carrying.
   - ❑ c. keep cooler.

8. You can conclude that lions are
   - ❑ a. feared by most other animals.
   - ❑ b. ignored by most other animals.
   - ❑ c. protected by most other animals.

9. You can conclude that lions usually avoid humans because people
   - ❑ a. are the enemies of lions.
   - ❑ b. are difficult to stalk.
   - ❑ c. are harder to hunt than herd animals.

10. Throughout history, humans have regarded lions as
    - ❑ a. pets.
    - ❑ b. fascinating creatures.
    - ❑ c. terrifying enemies.

The pride of lions was resting in tall grass in the heat of the day. Unaware of the lions, a herd of gazelles grazed peacefully not far off. Six female lions began moving slowly toward the herd. They walked through the two-foot-high (60-centimeter) grass with their heads low. One lion moved ahead a short way and lay down. Then in turn another lion moved. Each lion crept forward a little and then hid in the grass. Nothing showed above the grass. The gazelles did not seem aware of the lions' presence. They continued to graze. Now and then, a lion raised her head above the grass to look at the gazelles. She then lowered her head quickly to avoid being seen.

   The lions fanned out to form a semicircle with the herd at its center. They continued to edge closer and closer to the gazelles. When they were within striking distance, one lion charged. The panicked gazelles dashed in all directions! Several of them ran right at the waiting lions.

   Meanwhile, the other members of the pride sprang from their cover. Two male lions and a number of cubs of various sizes stood watching the hunt. When the lions had made their kill, the pride feasted.

1. Recognizing Words in Context

Find the word *pride* in the passage. One definition below is a *synonym* for that word; it means the same or almost the same thing. One definition is an *antonym;* it has the opposite or nearly opposite meaning. The other has a completely different meaning. Label the definitions S for *synonym*, A for *antonym*, and D for *different*.

_____ a. self-esteem

_____ b. group

_____ c. individual

2. Distinguishing Fact from Opinion

Two of the statements below present *facts*, which can be proved correct. The other statement is an *opinion*, which expresses someone's thoughts or beliefs. Label the statements F for *fact* and O for *opinion*.

_____ a. Male lions are lazy to let females do the hunting.

_____ b. Six lions moved toward the herd of gazelles.

_____ c. Two male lions and a number of cubs watched the hunt.

3. Keeping Events in Order

Label the statements below 1, 2, and 3 to show the order in which the events happened.

_____ a. The lions fanned out to form a semicircle with the gazelles at the center.

_____ b. The lions walked through the grass with their heads low.

_____ c. A pride of lions rested in the tall grass.

4. Making Correct Inferences

Two of the statements below are correct *inferences*, or reasonable guesses. They are based on information in the passage. The other statement is an incorrect, or faulty, inference. Label the statements C for *correct* inference and F for *faulty* inference.

_____ a. Female lions do most of the hunting for a pride of lions.

_____ b. The males in a pride of lions never do any hunting themselves.

_____ c. Lions work together when they hunt.

5. Understanding Main Ideas

One of the statements below expresses the main idea of the passage. One statement is too general, or too broad. The other explains only part of the passage; it is too narrow. Label the statements M for *main idea*, B for *too broad*, and N for *too narrow*.

_____ a. Several gazelles ran right at the waiting lions.

_____ b. Six lions cooperate to hunt and kill gazelles.

_____ c. The lion is one of the largest and strongest hunters in Africa.

Correct Answers, Part A _____

Correct Answers, Part B _____

Total Correct Answers _____

ANSWER KEY

READING RATE GRAPH

COMPREHENSION SCORE GRAPH

COMPREHENSION SKILLS PROFILE GRAPH

ANSWER KEY

1A	1. b	2. b	3. b	4. c	5. a	6. c	7. b	8. a	9. c	10. a
1B	1. S, A, D	2. F, O, F	3. S, S, A	4. C, F, C	5. M, B, N					
2A	1. a	2. c	3. b	4. c	5. c	6. b	7. c	8. a	9. a	10. c
2B	1. A, D, S	2. F, F, O	3. B, S, S	4. C, C, F	5. N, B, M					
3A	1. a	2. c	3. b	4. c	5. c	6. b	7. b	8. b	9. c	10. a
3B	1. D, S, A	2. F, F, O	3. S, A, S	4. C, C, F	5. B, N, M					
4A	1. b	2. b	3. a	4. c	5. b	6. b	7. b	8. a	9. a	10. c
4B	1. S, A, D	2. F, O, F	3. 1, 3, 2	4. C, C, F	5. N, M, B					
5A	1. a	2. b	3. b	4. c	5. a	6. c	7. a	8. b	9. b	10. b
5B	1. A, D, S	2. F, F, O	3. 2, 1, 3	4. F, C, C	5. B, N, M					
6A	1. b	2. a	3. b	4. a	5. b	6. c	7. c	8. b	9. c	10. c
6B	1. A, D, S	2. O, F, F	3. 2, 3, 1	4. C, F, C	5. M, N, B					
7A	1. a	2. c	3. c	4. b	5. b	6. a	7. c	8. b	9. a	10. b
7B	1. S, D, A	2. F, F, O	3. S, S, B	4. C, C, F	5. N, B, M					
8A	1. a	2. c	3. b	4. a	5. a	6. b	7. b	8. c	9. c	10. c
8B	1. S, A, D	2. F, F, O	3. 1, 3, 2	4. C, F, C	5. M, B, N					
9A	1. c	2. c	3. b	4. a	5. b	6. a	7. b	8. c	9. a	10. b
9B	1. D, A, S	2. F, O, F	3. B, S, S	4. F, C, C	5. B, N, M					
10A	1. c	2. b	3. c	4. c	5. b	6. a	7. b	8. a	9. c	10. a
10B	1. A, S, D	2. O, F, F	3. 3, 1, 2	4. C, F, C	5. N, B, M					
11A	1. a	2. b	3. b	4. c	5. c	6. a	7. c	8. c	9. b	10. b
11B	1. A, S, D	2. O, F, F	3. 3, 2, 1	4. F, C, C	5. M, B, N					
12A	1. b	2. b	3. a	4. c	5. b	6. a	7. c	8. a	9. b	10. c
12B	1. D, S, A	2. F, O, F	3. 2, 1, 3	4. F, C, C	5. B, N, M					
13A	1. b	2. c	3. b	4. a	5. c	6. c	7. b	8. a	9. b	10. a
13B	1. S, D, A	2. F, F, O	3. 2, 3, 1	4. C, C, F	5. M, N, B					

14A	1. a	2. c	3. a	4. b	5. c	6. b	7. a	8. a	9. c	10. c
14B	1. D, A, S	2. O, F, F	3. 1, 3, 2	4. F, C, C	5. N, M, B					
15A	1. a	2. b	3. c	4. b	5. a	6. b	7. a	8. c	9. a	10. a
15B	1. A, D, S	2. F, O, F	3. 1, 3, 2	4. F, C, C	5. M, B, N					
16A	1. c	2. a	3. a	4. b	5. b	6. b	7. a	8. c	9. c	10. b
16B	1. D, A, S	2. F, O, F	3. 3, 2, 1	4. F, C, C	5. M, B, N					
17A	1. c	2. b	3. a	4. a	5. b	6. c	7. b	8. a	9. c	10. a
17B	1. D, A, S	2. F, F, O	3. 2, 3, 1	4. F, C, C	5. N, M, B					
18A	1. b	2. a	3. b	4. c	5. b	6. c	7. b	8. b	9. b	10. c
18B	1. A, S, D	2. O, F, F	3. 2, 1, 3	4. C, F, C	5. B, M, N					
19A	1. a	2. b	3. b	4. c	5. c	6. b	7. a	8. c	9. c	10. a
19B	1. D, S, A	2. O, F, F	3. 3, 1, 2	4. C, C, F	5. N, M, B					
20A	1. b	2. c	3. a	4. b	5. c	6. a	7. a	8. c	9. b	10. c
20B	1. S, A, D	2. F, F, O	3. 1, 2, 3	4. C, C, F	5. B, M, N					
21A	1. a	2. b	3. c	4. b	5. a	6. a	7. b	8. b	9. c	10. a
21B	1. S, D, A	2. F, O, F	3. 2, 1, 3	4. C, C, F	5. B, N, M					
22A	1. b	2. c	3. c	4. b	5. a	6. a	7. b	8. c	9. a	10. c
22B	1. S, D, A	2. F, O, F	3. B, S, S	4. C, F, C	5. M, B, N					
23A	1. c	2. a	3. b	4. c	5. b	6. b	7. c	8. a	9. a	10. b
23B	1. A, D, S	2. O, F, F	3. S, S, B	4. C, F, C	5. N, B, M					
24A	1. b	2. a	3. c	4. a	5. b	6. a	7. b	8. c	9. c	10. c
24B	1. S, D, A	2. F, O, F	3. S, B, S	4. F, C, C	5. N, B, M					
25A	1. c	2. c	3. b	4. b	5. a	6. c	7. b	8. a	9. a	10. b
25B	1. D, S, A	2. O, F, F	3. 3, 2, 1	4. C, F, C	5. N, M, B					

Reading Rate

Put an X on the line above each lesson number to show your reading time and words-per-minute rate for that unit.

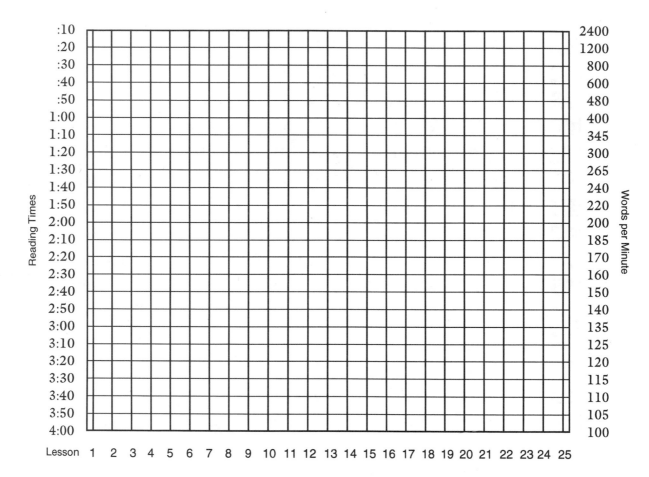

COMPREHENSION SCORE

Put an X on the line above each lesson number to indicate your total correct answers and comprehension score for that unit.

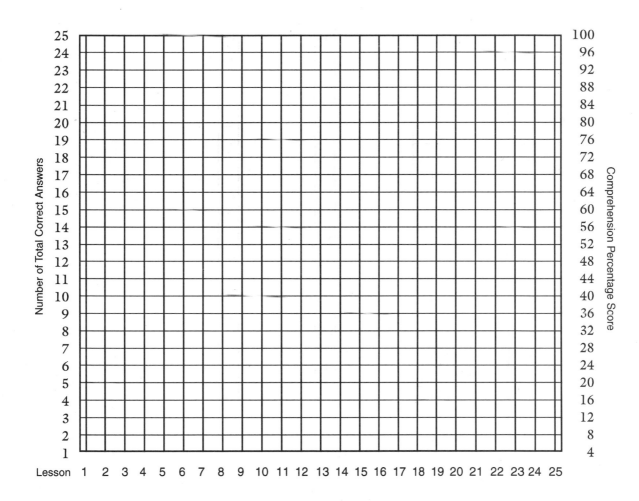

COMPREHENSION SKILLS PROFILE

Put an X in the box above each question type to indicate an incorrect reponse to any part of that question.

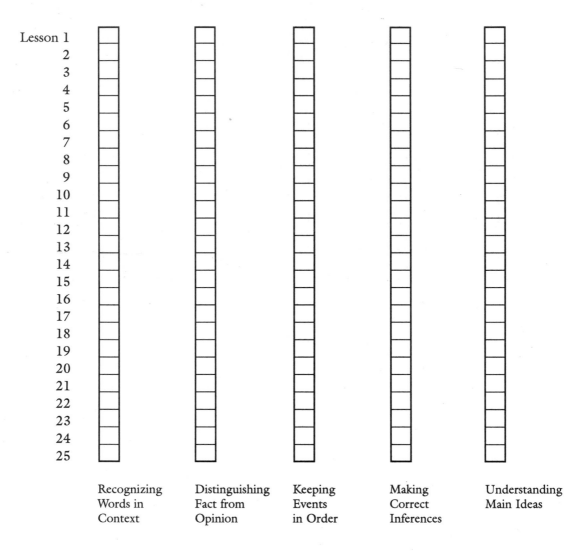

	Recognizing Words in Context	Distinguishing Fact from Opinion	Keeping Events in Order	Making Correct Inferences	Understanding Main Ideas
Lesson 1					
2					
3					
4					
5					
6					
7					
8					
9					
10					
11					
12					
13					
14					
15					
16					
17					
18					
19					
20					
21					
22					
23					
24					
25					